Chan Kwok Kin   Betty Hung

A Cantonese Book

Second Edition

Greenwood Press

GREENWOOD PRESS
47 Pokfulam Road, 8/F, Hong Kong.
Tel: 2546 8212
Fax: 2858 6042
Email: gwpress@ctimail.com

First published November, 2005.

ISBN-13: 978-962-279-248-7
ISBN-10: 962-279-248-0

PRINTED IN HONG KONG

Contents

Preface

"A Cantonese Book" is the second edition of a work which has been popular for over a decade. In 1994, "A Cantonese Book" was first published and soon was well-received by teachers and students all over the world. Their enthusiastic comments and suggestions have been incorporated into this new edition, which has new content and 3 CD's instead of cassettle tapes.

We hope these improvements will make this text even more convenient to use for our readers.

The book includes the following features:

1)   Characters are provided alongside their romanization so that Asian students and those who already know some characters can progress faster.

2)   The conversations are based on authentic situations. Expressions therein are idomatic while grammatical rules are also observed.

3)   New words are introduced step by step. Each lesson contains fewer than twenty new words. These new words constantly appear in the rest of the book.

4)   In the section on grammar, new words are introduced together with their parts of speech. Sentence patterns are analysed in their affirmative, negative and interrogative forms.

5)   Various exercises are set in each lesson. They include translation, questions and answers, filling in blanks, pyramid drills,

substitution drills, sentence construction, guided conversation, listening comprehension, etc.

6)   The glossary is given in two parts, namely, from Cantonese to English and from English to Cantonese. Students can therefore easily find and define each word.

7)   Appendices are attached to the end of the book. The appendix of Putonghua Equivalents of Cantonese Words directs students to do translation between Cantonese and Putonghua. The appendix of Cantonese slang helps students understand the slang expressions which dictionaries do not always contain.

Suggestions and comments are welcome.

How to use this book

This book is divided into 16 lessons.

Lessons 1-3 teach useful daily expressions like numbers, daily greetiings and directions for taxi and minibus drivers. These simple phrases encourage students to speak Cantonese in daily life and to pick up words commonly used around them.

In lessons 4-16, students start to learn basic Cantonese structures, as well as around 300 words or phrases. Each lesson is divided into the following sections:

1. **Conversation:** Topics are carefully chosen. The style is lively and close to daily life. Furthermore, the contents serve as a summary of the sentence pattern(s) of the lesson. In this way students can review and practise what they have learned in an interesting way. In some lessons, there are also passages to be read. The contents of the passages are mostly related to the conversation or serve as a summary of sentence patterns.

   If there are new vocabulary items, the English explanation follows in parentheses with an asterisk *.

   eg. dím-gáai (*why)

   Teachers should ask questions on each conversation to make sure students understand the contents.

2. **Vocabulary:** Around 15 words or phrases are introduced in each lesson. After the romanized form of vocabulary items, the

Chinese character is given. (Since Cantonese is a spoken dialect, there is actually no written form. We will, however, choose appropriate Chinese characters to represent them for easy reading.) In the right column of the vocabulaty section are parts of speech and English equivalents. Related phrases are introduced with an asterisk *.

eg. syù 書 (M: bùn 本)　　　　　N : book

　　* Yìng-màhn-syù 英文書 : English book

Abbreviations of parts of speech:

ADJ	adjective
ADV	adverb
AV	auxilary verb
CON	conjunction
FP	final particle
IE	idomatic expressions
M	measure
N	noun
NU	number
P	particle
Ph	phrase
PN	pronoun
PW	place word
QW	question word
SP	specifier
TW	time word
V	verb
VO	verb object compound
VS	verb suffix

3. **Sentence patterns:** These explain the grammatical structures with drills of the patterns. The structure is highlighted in a box. The affirmative, negative and question forms of the patterns are explained. In the pattern drills, the key word of the pattern is underlined. If there are some English words in the sentences, it is put in single quote markers.

    Teachers should explain the structures, then drill the students with the pattern sentences. Students should close the book and repeat the sentences after teachers. Students should be discouraged from reading sentences from the book. Teachers may also ask students to translate the sentences.

4. **Pyramid drills and substitution drills:** This is a review of sentence pattern(s) of the lesson.

5. **Review exercise:** The exercises contain both oral and written parts. Students should prepare the exercises before their class. For questions and answers, teachers should ask students to close the book and answer orally.

6. **Listening exercise:** Listen to the dialogues of the CD and answer the questions. In each lesson, there are around 12 questions.

    At the end of some lessons, there are related cultural notes. These notes make it more fun for students to learn Cantonese, and improve their understanding of the society of Hong Kong.

Romanization System

Each syllabus of Cantonese is composed of three elements:

1. Initial: the beginning sound element of a syllable. There are 19 initials in all.

2. Finial: the ending sound element of a syllable or a vowel. There are 51 finals in all.

3. Tone: the relative pitch, or variation of pitch, of a syllable. There are 7 tones in all.

An example of a syllable:

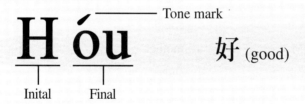

好 (good)

An example of a syllable:

你 (you)

INITIALS *(CD 1, Track 1)*

		as in English	*example*
1.	B	boy	ba
2.	P	park	pa
3.	D	dig	da
4.	T	till	ta
5.	G	game	ga
6.	K	kill	ka
7.	F	far	fa
8.	H	home	ha
9.	N	no	na
10.	L	law	la
11.	J	jam	ja
12.	Ch	check	cha
13.	M	mother	ma
14.	Ng	singer	nga
15.	Gw	language	gwa
16.	Kw	quite	kwa
17.	S	sand	sa
18.	W	water	wa
19.	Y	yes	ya

FINALS *(CD 1, Track 2)*

		as in English	example	(meaning)
AA				
1.	a	father	chā 叉	(fork)
2.	aai	aisle	saai 晒	(shine upon)
3.	aau	owl	gaau 教	(teach)
4.	aam	arm	sāam 衫	(clothes)
5.	aan	aunt	fàan 返	(return)
6.	aang	Hong Kong (American pronunciation)	sàang 生	(raw)
7.	aap	harp ("p" mute) (tongue not curled)	jaahp 閘	(gate)
8.	aat	art ("t" mute) (tongue not curled)	baat 八	(eight)
9.	aak	ark ("k" mute) (tongue not curled)	baak 百	(hundred)
A				
10.	ai	sight	sai 細	(samll)
11.	au	out ("t" mute)	gau 夠	(enough)
12.	am	sum	sām 心	(heart)
13.	an	sun	fàn 分	(minute)
14.	ang	dung	dáng 等	(wait)
15.	ap	up ("p" mute)	jāp 汁	(juice)
16.	at	but ("t" mute)	bāt 筆	(pen)
17.	ak	duck ("k" mute)	bāk 北	(north)

E

18.	e	yes	jē 遮	(umbrella)
19.	eng	leng	tèng 聽	(listen)
20.	ek	echo	sek 錫	(kiss)
21.	ei	day	béi 畀	(give)

EU

22.	eu	her	hèu 靴	(boot)
		(tongue not curled)		
23.	eung	ear (ni)ng	séung 想	(wish to)
24.	euk	turk ("k" mute)	jeuk 着	(wear)
		(tongue not curled)		
25.	eui	deuil (in French)	heui 去	(go)
26.	eun	(nat) ion	seun 信	(letter)
27.	eut	no equivalent	chēut 出	(out)

I

28.	i	bee	si 試	(try)
29.	iu	"ee" + "oo"	síu 少	(few)
30.	im	seem	dím 點	(o'clock)
31.	in	seen	sìn 先	(first)
32.	ip	jeep ("p" mute)	díp 碟	(dish)
33.	it	seat ("t" mute)	yiht 熱	(hot)
34.	ing	sing	bìng 冰	(ice)
35.	ik	sick ("k" mute)	sīk 識	(know)

O

36.	o	orchard	cho 錯	(wrong)
37.	oi	boy	choi 菜	(vegetables)
38.	on	on	gòn 乾	(dry)
39.	ong	song	tòng 湯	(soup)
40.	ot	ought ("t" mute)	hot 渴	(thirsty)
41.	ok	awkward ("k" mute)	gwok 國	(country)
42.	ou	toe	móuh 冇	(have not)

U

43.	u	fruit	fú 苦	(bitter)
44.	ui	"oo" + "ee"	bùi 杯	(cup)
45.	un	soon	wún 碗	(bowl)
46.	ut	boot ("t" mute)	fut 闊	(wide)
47.	ung	tongue (N. English)	jūng 鐘	(clock)
48.	uk	hook ("k" mute)	ūk 屋	(house)

YU

49.	yu	Dessus (in French)	syù 書	(book)
50.	yun	Une (in French)	syùn 酸	(sour)
51.	yut	chute (in French)	yuht 月	(month)

TONES   *(CD 1, Track 3)*

The following is a sketch illustrating the co-relation of the seven tones in Cantonese:

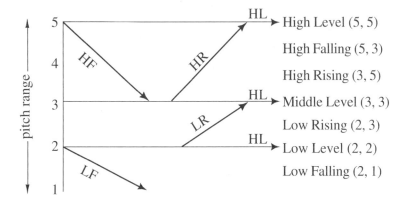

It is important to note that a sound in a certain tone may differ in meaning from the same sound in another tone. (The following is an example.)

Name of Tone	Tone mark	Example	
High Level	with '‾' on top of first vowel	sī	poem 詩
High Falling	with '`' on top of first vowel	sì	to tear 撕
High Rising	with '´' on top of first vowel	sí	history 史
Middle Level	none	si	to try 試
Low Falling	with '`' on top, an 'h' after the vowel(s)	sìh	time 時
Low Rising	with '´' on top, an 'h' after the vowel(s)	síh	market 市
Low Level	with an 'h' after the vowel(s)	sih	matter 事

SIMILAR INITIAL DRILL *(CD 1, Track 4)*

'b' and 'p'

1. báau 飽   páau 跑   4. bìng 冰   pìng 拼(盤)
2. bèi 卑   pèi 披   5. bok 搏   pok 撲
3. bài 跋   pài 批

'g' and 'k'

1. gāt 吉   kāt 咳   4. gèui 居   kèui 區
2. gèung 薑   kèuhng 強   5. géi 幾   kéi (屋)企
3. gìng 經   kìng 傾

'd' and 't'

1. dēng 釘   tēng 廳   4. dou 到   tou 套
2. diu 吊   tiu 跳   5. dung 凍   tung 痛
3. dyún 短   tyúhn 斷

'gw' and 'kw'

1. gwóng 廣   kwong 鄺   4. gwok 國   kwok 擴
2. gwài 歸   kwài 規   5. gwà 瓜   kwà 跨
3. gwaan 慣   kwaang 逛

'j' and 'ch'

1. jāp 汁   chāp 輯   4. jóu 早   chóu 草
2. jeung 醬   cheung 唱   5. jyun 轉   chyun 寸
3. jit 節   chit 切   6. jūk 捉   chūk 束

DIFFICULT INITIAL DRILLS   *(CD 1, Track 5)*

'y'

1. yàu 休	4. yèung 央	7. yiu 要
2. yèhng 贏	5. yeuih 銳	8. yīn 煙
3. yeuk 約	6. yeuhn 潤	9. yúk 玉

'ng'

1. ngàaih 捱	4. ngàhn 銀	7. ngāam 啱
2. ngàuh 牛	5. ngohk 鱷	8. ngúng
3. ngàih 危	6. ngouh 傲	9. ngáng

'n' and 'ng'

1. noh 糯	ngoh 餓	4. nouh 怒	ngouh 傲
2. ná 嬤	ngá 啞	5. nám 諗	ngám 黯
3. nok 諾	ngok 惡		

SIMILAR FINIAL DRILLS   *(CD 1, Track 6)*

'aa' and 'a'

1. chàai 猜	chài 妻	5. sàang 生	sàng 生(命)
2. gáam 減	gám 感	6. saahp 烚	sahp 十
3. māau 貓	māu 踎	7. waaht 滑	waht 核
4. wáan 玩	wán 搵	8. āak 握	āk 扼

'ing' and 'eng'

1. pìhng 瓶   pèhng 平   5. hìng 興(旺)   hèng 輕
2. dīng 丁   dēng 釘   6. jíng 整   jéng 井
3. tìng 聽   tēng 廳   7. líhng (引)領   léhng (衣)領
4. gíng 景   géng 頸   8. sìng 升   sèng 腥

'ek' and 'ik'

1. sehk 石   sihk 食   4. pek 劈   pīk 辟
2. tek 踢   tīk 剔   5. chek 尺   chīk 戚
3. jehk 蓆   jihk 直

'eng', 'ing' and 'in'

1. jèng 精(叻)   jìng 晶   jìn 煎
2. tēng 廳   tìng 聽(日)   tīn 天
3. chéng 請   chíng 拯   chín 錢
4. yèhng 贏   yìhng 仍   yìhn 然
5. behng 病   bihng 並   bihn 便

'euk', 'uk' and 'ok'

1. dēuk 跺   dūk 督   dohk (量)度
2. geuk 腳   gūk 菊   gok 角
3. jeuhk 着   juhk 續   johk 昨
4. leuhk 略   luhk 六   lohk 落
5. yeuhk 藥   yuhk 肉   wohk 鑊
6. seuk 削   suhk 熟   sok 索

'ong', 'eng' and 'ung'

1. hòng 康	hèung 香	hùng 空
2. gòng 剛	gèung 薑	gùng 工
3. kòhng 狂	kèuhng 強	kùhng 窮
4. jong 壯	jeung 醬	jung 眾
5. lòhng 狼	lèuhng 涼	lùhng 龍
6. sòng 桑	sèung 雙	sùng 鬆
7. chóng 廠	chéung 腸	chúng 寵

'o' and 'ou'

1. dò 多	dōu 都	4. jó 左	jóu 早
2. tóh 妥	tóuh 肚	5. cho 錯	chou 醋
3. go 個	gou 告		

'e' and 'ei'

1. bē 啤(酒)	bèi 卑	4. dé 嗲	déi (質)地
2. péh	péih 被	5. mē 咩	mēi (第)尾
3. ké 茄	kéi (屋)企		

'it' and 'ik'

1. jiht 截	jihk 直	4. dīt 啲(多)	dīk 的
2. yiht 熱	yihk 亦	5. miht 滅	mihk 覓
3. chit 切	chīk 戚		

'eut' and 'euk'

1. chēut 出	cheuk 卓	3. leuht 律	leuhk 略
2. jēut 卒	jeuk 雀	4. sēut 恤	seuk 削

'eun' and 'eung'

1. yeuhn 潤	yeuhng 樣	4. jéun 準	jéung 奬
2. chèun 春	chēung 窗	5. dēun 敦	dēung
3. seun 信	seung 相		

'-n' and '-ng'

1. sàn 新	sàng 生(命)	5. jaahn 賺	jaahng
2. bàn 賓	bàng 崩	6. maahn 萬	maahng 孟
3. jàn 眞	jàng 憎	7. gón 趕	góng 講
4. sàan 山	sàang 生	8. hòn 看(護)	hòng 康

TONE DRILLS   *(CD 1, Track 7)*

1. sìn-sàang 先生
   fàan-gùng 返工
   chà-sìu 叉燒

2. kìng-gái 傾偈
   Hèung-góng 香港
   chèun-gyún 春卷

3. tìn-hei 天氣
   jùng-yi 鍾意
   Yìng-gwok 英國

4. sìng-kèih 星期
   Jùng-wàahn 中環
   fàan làih 返嚟

5. tìng-máahn 聽晚
    gàai-síh 街市
    jyù-láuh 豬柳

6. yàn-waih 因爲
    dò-jeh 多謝
    gàm-yaht 今日

7. hóu-tìn 好天
    síu-sàm 小心
    jóu-fàn 早婚

8. dím-gáai 點解
    géi dím 幾點
    síu-jé 小姐

9. tái hei 睇戲
    gó go 嗰個
    jáu-dim 酒店

10. géi-sìh 幾時
    Gáu-lùhng 九龍
    jáu-làuh 酒樓

11. tái-háh 睇碡
    hó-yíh 可以
    só-yíh 所以

12. chéng mahn 請問
    jó-mihn 左面
    cháau faahn 炒飯

13. daap līp 搭粒
    gei-dāk 記得
    jyun wāan 轉彎

14. bou-jí 報紙
    taai-táai 太太
    dung séui 凍水

15. fong-ga 放假
    gwai sing 貴姓
    fan-gaau 瞓覺

16. m̀h-gòi 唔該
    hùhng-sīk 紅色
    yìh-gā 而家

17. mùhn-háu 門口
    làih-jó 嚟咗
    yùh-gwó 如果

18. chìh-dou 遲到
    sìhng-haak 乘客
    làih-gwo 嚟過

19. sìh-sìh 時時
    pìhng-sìh 平時
    tùhng-màaih 同埋

20. kàhm-máahn 琴晚
    pàhng-yáuh 朋友
    m̀h-máaih 唔買

21. tùhng-sih 同事
    chìhn-mihn 前面
    hàahng-louh 行路

22. máaih syù 買書
    Méih-sàm 美心
    léuhng màn 兩蚊

23. Néih hóu 你好
    ngóh gwú 我估
    máaih-dóu 買倒

24. ngáahn-fan 眼瞓
    láih-baai 禮拜
    ńgh chi 五次

25. náaih-chàh 奶茶
    yáuh-sìh 有時
    léuih-hàhng 旅行

26. yáuh móuh 有冇
    máaih yéh 買嘢
    móuh yéh 冇嘢

27. tóuh-ngoh 肚餓
    néih-deih 你哋
    kéuih-deih 佢哋

28. dihn-wá 電話
    Yaht-bún 日本
    deih-há 地下

29. sahp baat 十八
    sihk aan 食晏
    deih-tit 地鐵

30. yih sahp 二十
    hauh-mihn 後面
    dihn-sih 電視

Number 0 To 99

(CD 1, Track 8)

romanization	Chinese character	hand signs
1 yāt	一	
2 yih	二	
3 sàam	三	
4 sei	四	

romanization	Chinese character	hand signs
5 ńgh or ḿh	五	
6 luhk	六	
7 chāt	七	
8 baat	八	
9 gáu	九	
10 sahp	十	
0 lìhng	零	

11 – 20

11	sahp yāt 十一	16	sahp luhk 十六
12	sahp yih 十二	17	sahp chāt 十七
13	sahp sàam 十三	18	sahp baat 十八
14	sahp sei 十四	19	sahp gáu 十九
15	sahp ńgh 十五	20	yih sahp 二十

21 – 99

20 yih sahp   二十..... 29 yih sahp gáu 二十九/yah gáu 廿九

30 sàam sahp 三十..... 39 sàam sahp gáu 三十九/sà-ah gáu 卅九

40 sei sahp   四十..... 49 sei sahp gáu/sei-ah gáu 四十九

50 ńgh sahp   五十..... 59 ńgh sahp gáu/ńgh-ah gáu 五十九

60 luhk sahp 六十..... 69 luhk sahp gáu/luhk-ah gáu 六十九

70 chāt sahp 七十..... 79 chāt sahp gáu/chāt-ah gáu 七十九

80 baat sahp 八十..... 89 baat sahp gáu/baat-ah gáu 八十九

90 gáu sahp   九十..... 99 gáu sahp gáu/gáu-ah gáu 九十九

EXERCISE

I.   Read the following numbers

1. 19	6. 39	11. 35	16. 51
2. 64	7. 14	12. 76	17. 63
3. 87	8. 21	13. 49	18. 16
4. 93	9. 85	14. 28	19. 57

II.   Read the following calculations and give answers

1. 12 + 9
    sahp yih gà gáu haih
    十　二　加　九　係

2. 5 + 7

3. 8 + 35

4. 51 + 3

5. 13 + 29

6. 2 × 8
    yih sìhng baat haih
    二　乘　八　係

7. 9 × 7

8. 5 × 12

9. 8 × 7

10. 46 × 6

11. 97 − 5
    gáu sahp chāt gáam ńgh haih
    九　十　七　減　五　係

12. 41 − 2

13. 76 − 4

14. 83 − 6

15. 58 − 1

16. 63 ÷ 7
    chāt chèuih luhk sahp sàam haih
    七　除　六　十　三　係

17. 54 ÷ 9

18. 42 ÷ 6

19. 35 ÷ 5

20. 72 ÷ 8

Toboos and popular beliefs about numbers

Lucky numbers

二   sounds the same as easy (yùhng-yih 容易).

三   sounds like lively, energetic (sàang-máahng 生猛).

八   sounds like prosperous and making money (faat 發 /
     faat-daaht 發達 /faat-chòih 發財).

九   sounds the same as long-lasting (chèuhng-gáu 長久).

UnLucky numbers

四   sounds like to die (séi 死). Fourteen and twenty four
are not welcomed by Hong Kong people either. Fourteen sounds like 'saht séi' 「實死」which means
to die certainly. Twenty four sounds like easy to die
(yih séi 易死). Many buildings in Hong Kong have
no thirteenth (western unlucky number) and fourteenth
(Cantonese unlucky number) floors.

七   is not welcomed by people, because this is a number
which is used in Chinese funerals. Moreover, the
pronunciation of 'chāt' sounds the same as a vulgar
Cantonese word.

Lesson 2

Useful Daily Expressions

(CD 1, Track 9)

1. Néih hóu. 你好。 Good day! / How do you do?

2. Jóu-sàhn. 早晨。 Good morning!

3. Jóu-táu. 早抖。 Good night!

4. Bāai-baai. 拜拜。 Bye!

> There is no greeting similar to "Good afternoon" and "Good evening".

5. M̀h-gòi dáng dáng. 唔該等等。/ Wait a moment, please.
   M̀h-gòi dáng jahn. 唔該等陣。

Thanks for someone's help or service

6. *A:* M̀h-gòi (saai). 唔該(晒)。 Thank you very much.

   B: M̀h-sái (m̀h-gòi). 唔駛(唔該)。 You're welcome.

> M̀h-gòi 「唔該」 can also mean 'Excuse me' or 'Please' as in "please make way".

Thanks for someone's help or service

7. *A:* Dò-jeh (saai).   Thank you
        多謝(晒)。   very much.

    B: M̀h-sái (dò-jeh).   Not at all.
        唔駛(多謝)。

> Dò-jeh「多謝」is also the
> reply to congratulations,
> invitations, or expressions
> of appreciation.

When you apologize for being late

8. *A:* M̀h-hóu yi-sì. Ngóh chìh-dou.   Sorry, I'm late.
        唔 好 意 思 。 我 遲 到 。

    B: M̀h-gán-yiu. 唔 緊 要 。   Never mind.

REVIEW EXERCISE

What do you say when......

1. someone opens the door for you.

2. you greet someone at 8:00 a.m.

3. someone thanks you for your help.

4. someone presses the button for you in an elevator.

5. you are late.

6. asking your friend to wait a moment.

7. someone apologizes to you.

8. you drop your keys and someone picks them up for you.

9. someone congratulates you on your promotion.

10. you leave home for work.

11. you bump into somebody.

12. you leave the office.

Lesson 3

Turn Left And Stop Please

CONVERSATION   *(CD 1, Track 10)*

A.

 M̀h-gòi, deih-tit jaahm hái bīn-douh a?

唔 該 ， 地 鐵 站 喺 邊 度 呀 ？

Excuse me, where is the MTR station?

Jihk heui, gāai-háu jyun jó jauh haih la.

直 去 ， 街 口 轉 左 就 係 喇 。

Go straight, turn left at the street junction, and there it is.

M̀h-gòi-saai.

唔 該 晒 。

Thank you.

> **MTR**
> Mass Transit Railway
> (underground railway)

M̀h-sái.

唔 駛 。

You're welcome.

B.   *(CD 1, Track 11)*

Jóu-sàhn. Néih heui bīn-douh a?

早 晨 。 你 去 邊 度 呀 ？

Good morning. Where are you going?

Ngóh heui Wāan-jái. Néih nē?
我 去 灣 仔 。 你 呢 ?
I'm going to Wan Chai. What about you?

Ngóh heui Jùng-wàahn.
我 去 中 環 。
I'm going to Central.

Néih daap māt-yéh chè a?
你 搭 乜 嘢 車 呀 ?
What form of transport are you taking?

Ngóh daap dīk-sí. Néih nē?
我 搭 的 士 。 你 呢 ?
I'll take a taxi. And you?

Ngóh daap deih tit. Bāai-baai.
我 搭 地 鐵 。 拜 拜 。
I'll take the MTR. Bye.

Joi-gin.
再 見 。
See you again.

USEFUL VOCABULARY   *(CD 1, Track 12)*

1. jihk heui 直去   Ph : go straight

2. jyun jó 轉左   VO : turn left

3. jyun yauh 轉右   VO : turn right

4. bīn-douh 邊度   QW : where

5. nī-douh 呢度   Ph : here

6. gó-douh 嗰度   Ph : there

7. tìhng 停   V : stop

Drill

   a. Nī-douh tìhng. 呢度停。   Stop here.

   b. Chìhn-mihn tìhng. 前面停。   Stop there (in front).

   c. Jyun jó tìhng. 轉左停。   Turn left and stop.

   d. Gāai-háu tìhng. 街口停。   Stop at the street junction.

8. yáuh lohk 有落   Ph : stop (used on minibuses only)

Drill

   a. Nī-douh yáuh lohk.   Stop here.
      呢度有落。

   b. Chìhn-mihn yáuh lohk.   Stop there (in front).
      前面有落。

   c. Jyun jó yáuh lohk.   Turn left and stop.
      轉左有落。

   d. Dāng-wái yáuh lohk.   Stop at the traffic lights.
      燈位有落。

   e. Gwo-jó dāng-wái yáuh   Stop after the lights.
      lohk. 過咗燈位有落。

   f. Gāai-háu yáuh lohk.   Stop at the (street) junction.
      街口有落。

   g. Sih-dàan-leih Gāai yáuh   Stop at Stanley Street.
      lohk. 士丹利街有落。

   h. Yàuh-jaahm yáuh lohk.   Stop at the gasoline station.
      油站有落。

   i. Baak-gàai yáuh lohk.   Stop at the Park'n Shop.
      百佳有落。

   j. Gaau-tóng yáuh lohk.   Stop at the church.
      教堂有落。

EXERCISE

I.   Using the sketch map below, give directions for how to walk from one place to another.

eg. Car Park to Shopping Centre:

jyun jó jihk heui 轉左直去

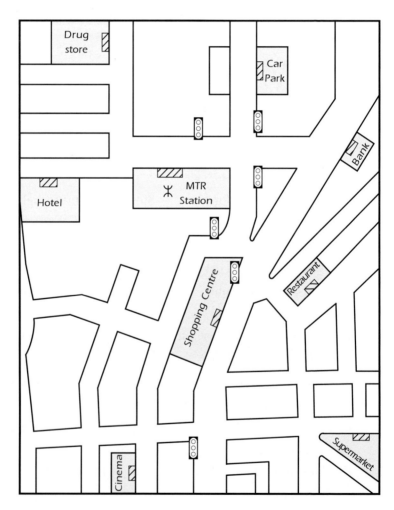

Bank	ngàhn-hòhng 銀行
Car Park	tìhng-chè-chèuhng 停車場
Cinema	hei-yún 戲院
Drug Store	yeuhk fòhng 藥房
Hotel	jáu-dim 酒店
MTR Station	deih-tit jaahm 地鐵站
Restaurant	chāan-tēng 餐廳
Shopping Centre	sèung-chèuhng 商場
Supermarket	chìu-kāp-síh-chèuhng 超級市場

1. Bank to Shopping Centre

2. MTR Station to Restaurant

3. Hotel to Cinema

4. Drug Store to Hotel

5. Supermarket to Car Park

6. Cinema to Bank

7. Shopping Centre to Drug Store

8. Restaurant to MTR Station

II. What transport do you take? *(CD 1, Track 13)*

Néih daap māt-yéh chè a? (What transport do you take?)
你　搭　乜　嘢　車　呀？

⇨　Ngóh daap dīk-sí. (I take a taxi.)
　　我　搭　的　士　。

⇨   Ngóh jà-chè. (I drive.)
    我　揸　車　。

⇨   Ngóh hàahng-louh. (I walk.)
    我　行　路　。

Transportations

- dīk-sí 的士   taxi
- síu-bā 小巴   mini bus
- bā-sí 巴士   bus
- deih-tit 地鐵   MTR (underground railway)
- fó-chè 火車   KCR (train)
- syùhn 船   ferry, boat
- laahm-chè 纜車   peak tram
- dihn-chè 電車   tram

MTR announcements

Chéng-maht kaau-gahn chè-mùhn.   Please keep clear of the
請　勿　靠　近　車　門　。   doors.

Chéng síu-sàm chè-mùhn.   Mind the doors please.
請　小　心　車　門　。

Hah-yāt jaahm Tùhng-lòh-wāan.   The next station, Cause-
下　一　站　銅　鑼　灣　。   way Bay.

Lesson 4

He Is My Friend

A. Miss Chan meets Mr Wong for the first time and they exchange business cards

Gwai sing a?
貴 姓 呀？
May I know your name?

Ngóh haih Wòhng Gwok-gèi. Néih hóu.
Nī-go haih ngóh kāat-pín.
我 係 黃 國 基 。 你 好 。
呢 個 係 我 卡 片 。
My name is Wong Kwok Kei. How do you do?
This is my business card.

> "ngóh kāat-pín"
> is short for "ngóh
> ge kāat-pín"

Dò-jeh. Ngóh haih Chàhn Mìhng-sī. Nī-go haih ngóh
kāat-pín.
多 謝 。 我 係 陳 明 詩 。 呢 個 係 我
卡 片 。
Thank you. My name is Chan Ming Si. This is my card.

B.   Mr Wong and Miss Chan meet on the street, and he introduces her to his wife. *(CD 1, Track 15)*

Hāai!   Wòhng sàang, hóu-noih-móuh-gin.
Néih dím a?
嗨！黃 生，好 耐 冇 見。
你 點 呀？
Hi! Mr Wong, haven't seen you for a
long time. How are you?

> "Wòhng sàang" is a short form of "Wòhng sìn-sàang"

Ngóh géi hóu.   Néih nē?
我 幾 好。 你 呢？
I'm fine. And you?

Ngóh dōu géi hóu.
我 都 幾 好。
I'm fine too.

Dáng ngóh làih gaai-siuh,
kéuih haih ngóh taai-táai.
等 我 嚟 介 紹。
佢 係 我 太 太。
Let me introduce.
She is my wife.

> "ngóh taat-táai" is a short form of "ngóh ge taai-táai"

Wòhng táai, néih hóu.   Ngóh haih Chàhn Mìhng-sī.
黃 太！ 你 好。 我 係 陳 明 詩。
Mrs Wong, nice to meet you. I'm Chan Ming Si.

Chàhn síu-jé, néih hóu.
陳 小 姐，你 好。
Miss Chan, nice to meet you.

> "Wòhng táai" is a short form of "Wòhng taat-táai"

VOCABULARY   *(CD 1, Track 16)*

1. ngóh 我   PN : I; me

2. néih or léih 你   PN : you

3. kéuih 佢   PN : he; him; she; her; it

4. ngóh-deih 我哋   PN : we, us

5. néih-deih or   PN : you (plural)
   léih-deih 你哋

6. kéuih-deih 佢哋   PN : they, them

7. sìn-sàang 先生   N : Mr; husband; teacher
   eg. Chàhn (sìn)-sàang 陳(先)生 : Mr Chan

8. síu-jé 小姐   N : Miss
   eg. Wòhng síu-jé 黃小姐 : Miss Wong

9. taai-táai 太太   N : Mrs; wife; lady (married)
   eg. Chàhn (taai)-táai 陳(太)太 : Mrs Chan

10. pàhng-yáuh 朋友   N : friend

11. tùhng-sih 同事   N : colleague

12. kāat-pín 卡(咭)片   N : thirsty

13. ge 嘅   P : indicating modification

14. go 個   M : used for counting people and
                            many other objects

15. wái 位   M : a polite form to count people

16. dī 啲   M : indicating plural form or
                            uncountable

17. nī or lī 呢   SP : this

　　eg. nī-go 呢個 : this one

　　　　nī-dī 呢啲 : these

18. gó 嗰   SP : that

　　eg. gó-go 嗰個 : that one

　　　　gó-dī 嗰啲 : those

19. bīn 邊   SP : used with measure to become
　　　　　　　　　　　　　　　which, who, whom, where

　　eg. bīn-go 邊個 : which one; who

　　　　bīn-dī 邊啲 : which of these

20. haih 係   V : equal; verb to be

21. m̀h 唔   P : not

SENTENCE PATTERNS   *(CD 1, Track 17)*

A. People qualifying people

☞ ____ (+ ge/ dī) + noun :   noun of ____, noun's ____
　____ （+ 嘅／啲）+ 名詞

　　eg. Ngóh ge pàhng-yáuh 我嘅朋友 : My friend(s)

　　　　Ngóh dī pàhng-yáuh 我啲朋友 : My friends

1. Ngóh ge taai-táai 我嘅太太　　My wife

2. Kéuih ge tùhng-sih 佢嘅同事　　His (or her) colleagues

3. Pàhng-yáuh ge pàhng-yáuh　　Friend's friend(s)
　　朋友嘅朋友

4. Wòhng sàang ge taai-táai   Mr Wong's wife
   黃生嘅太太

5. Néih dī pàhng-yáuh 你啲朋友   Your friends

6. Kéuih dī tùhng-sih 佢啲同事   His (or her) colleagues

7. Chàhn táai dī pàhng-yáuh   Mrs Chan's friends
   陳太啲朋友

8. Kéuih taai-táai 佢太太   His wife

9. Néih pàhng-yáuh 你朋友   Your friend(s)

10. Ngóh kāat-pín 我卡片   My business card

B.   Specifying people or objects *(CD 1, Track 18)*

☞   Specifier + measure + noun   指定詞＋量詞＋名詞

    eg. Nī-go pàhng-yáuh 呢個朋友   : this friend

        Gó-go pàhng-yáuh 嗰個朋友   : that friend

        Nī-dī pàhng-yáuh 呢啲朋友   : these friends

        Gó-dī pàhng-yáuh 嗰啲朋友   : those friends

        Bīn-go pàhng-yáuh 邊個朋友 : which friend

        Bīn-dī pàhng-yáuh 邊啲朋友 : which group of
                                     friends

1. Nī-dī tùhng-sih 呢啲同事   These colleagues

2. Gó-wái taai-táai 嗰位太太   That madam

3. Bīn-dī tùhng-sih 邊啲同事   Which group of colleagues

4. Nī-wái síu-jé 呢位小姐   This young lady

5. Gó-go kāat-pín 嗰個卡片   That business card

PRACTICE

Choose the correct answer

1. She is your wife. : Kéuih haih néih ＿＿＿＿ taai-táai.
   佢　係　你 ＿＿＿＿＿ 太　太 ？

   a) ge 嘅   *b)* dī 啲   *c)* bīn 邊

2. His colleague is my friend. : Kéuih ＿＿＿＿ tùhng-sih haih ngóh
   pàhng-yáuh.
   佢 ＿＿＿＿＿ 同　事　係　我　朋　友 。

   a) ngóh 我   *b)* ✕   *c)* dī 啲

3. My friends are late. : Ngóh ＿＿＿＿ pàhng-yáuh chìh-dou.
   我 ＿＿＿＿＿ 朋　友　遲　到 。

   a) haih 係   *b)* go 個   *c)* ge 嘅

4. That colleague's surname is Wong. :
   Gó ＿＿＿＿ tùhng-sih sing Wòhng.
   嗰 ＿＿＿＿＿ 同　事　姓　黃 。

   a) ✕   *b)* go 個   *c)* dī 啲

5. This is our boss. : Nī- ＿＿＿＿ haih ngóh-deih bō-sí.
   呢 ＿＿＿＿＿ 係　我　哋　波　士 。

   a) wái 位   *b)* ge 嘅   *c)* ngóh 我

6. He is not my husband. : Kéuih m̀h-haih ngóh ＿＿＿＿ sìn-sàang.
   佢 ＿＿＿＿＿ 唔　係　我　先　生 。

   a) ✕   *b)* dī 啲   *c)* deih 哋

7.　I am waiting for my wife. : Ngóh dáng ngóh ____ taai-táai.

　　　　　　　　　　　　　　　我　等　我 ____　太　太 。

　　a)　Kéuih 佢　　b)　dī 啲　　　　c)　ge 嘅

8.　His wife's surname is Ho. : Kéuih ____ taai-táai sing Hòh.

　　　　　　　　　　　　　　　佢 ____　太　太　姓　何 。

　　a)　✗　　　　　b)　néih 你　　c)　bīn-go 邊個

C.　Verb to be : 'haih' 係　(CD 1, Track 19)

Affirmative statement :

☞　Noun 1 + haih + Noun 2　　　Noun 1 = Noun 2
　　名詞 1 ＋ 係 ＋ 名詞 2

eg. Kéuih haih Chàhn sìn-sàang.
　　佢　係　陳　先　生 。
　　(He is Mr Chan.)

Negative statement :

☞　Noun 1 + m̀h haih + Noun 2　　Noun 1 ≠ Noun 2
　　名詞 1 ＋ 唔係 ＋ 名詞 2

eg. Kéuih m̀h-haih Chàhn sìn-sàang.
　　佢　唔　係　陳　先　生 。
　　(He is not Mr Chan.)

Question form :

☞　Noun 1 + haih m̀h-haih + Noun 2 + a?
　　名詞 1 ＋ 係唔係 ＋ 名詞 2 ＋ 呀 ？

eg. Kéuih haih m̀h-haih Chàhn sìn-sàang a?

佢 係 唔 係 陳 先 生 呀 ？

(Is he Mr Chan?)

Answer: Haih. / M̀h-haih. 係 。 / 唔 係 。

(Yes. / No.)

1. Ngóh haih Wòhng Gwok-gèi.

   我 係 黃 國 基 。

2. Kéuih haih Chàhn sàang ge pàhng-yáuh.

   佢 係 陳 生 嘅 朋 友 。

3. Néih m̀h-haih kéuih-deih tùhng-sih.

   你 唔 係 佢 哋 同 事 。

4. Wòhng táai m̀h-haih ngóh pàhng-yáuh.

   黃 太 唔 係 我 朋 友 。

5. Kéuih haih ngóh taai-táai.

   佢 係 我 太 太 。

6. Chàhn sàang haih kéuih pàhng-yáuh,
   m̀h-haih kéuih sìn-sàang.

   陳 生 係 佢 朋 友 ，
   唔 係 佢 先 生 。

   > "sìn-sàang" can refer to someone's husband or teacher

7. Kéuih-deih haih m̀h-haih néih tùhng-sih a?

   佢 哋 係 唔 係 你 同 事 呀 ？

8. Kéuih haih m̀h-haih Wòhng sìn-sàang ge pàhng-yáuh a?

   佢 係 唔 係 黃 先 生 嘅 朋 友 呀 ？

9. Mìhng-sī m̀h-haih ngóh pàhng-yáuh.

   明 詩 唔 係 我 朋 友 。

10. Nī-go haih ngóh kāat-pín.

    呢 個 係 我 卡 片 。

PYRAMID DRILLS *(CD 1, Track 20)*

Chàhn Gà-mìhng
陳　家　明

haih Chàhn Gà-mìhng
係　陳　家　明

Kéuih haih Chàhn Gà-mìhng
佢　係　陳　家　明

Kéuih m̀h-haih Chàhn Gà-mìhng
佢　唔　係　陳　家　明

Kéuih m̀h-haih néih pàhng-yáuh Chàhn Gà-mìhng
佢　唔　係　你　朋　友　陳　家　明

Kéuih haih m̀h-haih néih pàhng-yáuh Chàhn Gà-mìhng a?
佢　係　唔　係　你　朋　友　陳　家　明　呀？

SUBSTITUTION DRILLS *(CD 1, Track 21)*

1. Kéuih haih Wòhng sìn-sàang. 佢係黃先生。

   a) ngóh taai-táai   *b)* Wòhng síu-jé ge pàhng-yáuh
       我太太   黃小姐嘅朋友

   c) Chàhn Mìhng-sī   *d)* Chàhn táai ge tùhng-sih
       陳明詩   陳太嘅同事

2. Néih haih m̀h-haih kéuih tùhng-sih a? 你係唔係佢同事呀？

   a) Wòhng Gwok-gèi 黃國基   *b)* Wòhng síu-jé 黃小姐
   c) kéuih pàhng-yáuh 佢朋友   *d)* Chàhn táai 陳太

REVIEW EXERCISE

I.   Fill in the blanks

1. Ngóh _____ Wòhng Mìhng-sī.

    我 _____ 黃 明 詩 。

2. Kéuih haih néih _____ .

    佢 係 你 _____ 。

3. Hòh sìn-sàang _____ -haih ngóh tùhng-sih.

    何 先 生 _____ 係 我 同 事 。

4. Chàhn táai _____ néih pàhng-yáuh _____ ?

    陳 太 _____ 你 朋 友 _____ ?

5. Ngóh haih _____ .

    我 係 _____ 。

II.   Translation

1. Are they Mr Ho's colleagues? (Ho = Hòh 何).

2. Is she your wife?

3. Miss Chan is not the friend of Mrs Wong.

4. She is their friend, not my colleague.

LISTENING EXERCISE   *(CD 1, Track 22)*

I.   Multiple Choice

1. Mrs Chan   _____

2. My colleague   _____

3. Their friend   _____

4. Your husband   _____

II.   Use the given information, give true and false to the statements on the CD.

> Mr Chan is the colleague of Miss Ho and Mrs Lee.
>
> Mr. Wong is the husband of Miss Ho.
>
> Mr Wong and the husband of Mrs Lee are friend.
>
> Ji-ming is the friend of Mr Chan.

(Chan : Chàhn 陳   Ho : Hòh 何   Lee : Léih 李

  Wong : Wòhng 王   Ji-ming : Ji-mìhng 志明)

1. _____   2. _____   3. _____   4. _____

5. _____   6. _____   7. _____

Lesson 5

What's Your Phone Number?

CONVERSATION   *(CD 1, Track 23)*

Wái, m̀h-gòi Chàhn sàang.
喂，唔 該 陳 生 。
Hello, may I speak to Mr Chan?

Néih dá-cho la.
你 打 錯 喇 。
You've dialed the wrong number.

(Mr Ho dials again.)

Wái, m̀h-gòi Chàhn sàang.
喂，唔 該 陳 生 。
Hello, may I speak to Mr Chan?

> "Bīn-wái" is a polite form of 'bīn-go 邊個' for asking who

Kéuih m̀h-hái douh.   Bīn-wái wán kéuih a?
佢 唔 喺 度 。 邊 位 搵 佢 呀 ？
He's not here. May I know who's calling?

Ngóh haih Hòh Gā-màhn.
我 係 何 家 文 。
I'm Ho Ka Man.

Chéng néih chìh-dī dá-làih lā.

請 你 遲 啲 打 嚟 啦 。

Could you call later please?

Mh-gòi néih giu kéuih dá dihn-wá béi ngóh lā.

唔 該 你 叫 佢 打 電 話 畀 我 啦 。

Please ask him to call me.

Néih géi-dō houh dihn-wá a?

你 幾 多 號 電 話 呀 ？

What's your phone number?

Ngóh dihn-wá haih 25778462.

我 電 話 係 25778462 。

My number is 25778462.

> "Ngóh dihn-wá" is a
> short form of "Ngóh ge
> dihn-wá" 我嘅電話

Mh-gòi saai. Bāai-baai.

唔 該 晒 。 拜 拜 。

Thank you. Bye

Bāai-baai.

拜 拜 。

Bye.

VOCABULARY   *(CD 1, Track 24)*

1. géi(-dō) houh 幾（多）號   QW : what number

2. dihn-wá 電話 (M: go 個)   N : telephone

3. dá dihn-wá 打電話   VO : make telephone calls

4. ūk-kéi 屋企   N : home

5. gūng-sī 公司   N : company; office

6. sáu-tàih dihn-wá 手提電話   PH : mobile phone

SENTENCE PATTERNS   *(CD 1, Track 25)*

A. Asking phone numbers

> *To ask a phone number:*
>
> *eg.* Neih géi-dō houh dihn-wá a?
> 你 幾 多 號 電 話 呀 ?
> (What's your telephhone number?)
>
> Ngóh dihn-wá haih 2387 2560.
> 我 電 話 係 2387 2560。
> (My phone number is 2387 2560.)

suggested answer:

1. Néih tùhng-sih ūk-kéi géi-dō houh dihn-wá a?   2877 3628
   你 同 事 屋 企 幾 多 號 電 話 呀 ?

2. Wòhng táai ge sáu-tàih dihn-wá géi-dō houh a?   9982 0031
   黃 太 嘅 手 提 電 話 幾 多 號 呀 ?

3. Néih ūk-kéi géi-dō houh dihn-wá a?   3421 7333
   你 屋 企 幾 多 號 電 話 呀 ?

4. Néih gūng-sī géi-dō houh dihn-wá a?   2756 7876
   你 公 司 幾 多 號 電 話 呀 ?

5. Néih pàhng-yàuh ūk-kéi géi-dō houh dihn-wá   2395 6059
   a?
   你 朋 友 屋 企 幾 多 號 電 話
   呀 ?

6. Kéuih pàhng-yàuh dihn-wá géi-dō houh a?   6576 3811
   佢 朋 友 電 話 幾 多 號 呀 ?

B.   Who are you calling?   *(CD 1, Track 26)*

☞   Person A + dá dihn-wá béi + Person B
　　人 A　 +　打 電 話 畀　 +　 人 B

　　eg. Néih dá dihn-wá béi ngóh.
　　　　你 打 電 話 畀 我 。
　　　　(You call me.)

☞   Person + dá dihn-wá béi bīn-go a?
　　人　 +　打 電 話 畀 邊 個 呀 ？

　　eg. Néih dá dihn-wá béi bīn-go a?
　　　　你 打 電 話 畀 邊 個 呀 ？
　　　　(Who are you calling?)

☞   Bīn-go dá dihn-wá béi + Person + a?
　　邊 個 打 電 話 畀　 +　 人　 +　 呀 ？

　　eg. Bīn-go dá dihn-wá béi néih a?
　　　　邊 個 打 電 話 畀 你 呀 ？
　　　　(Who called you? / Who is calling you?)

1.   Ngóh dá dihn-wá béi ngóh pàhng-yáuh.
　　我 打 電 話 畀 我 朋 友 。

2.   Bīn-go dá dihn-wá béi Chàhn sìn-sàang a?
　　邊 個 打 電 話 畀 陳 先 生 呀 ？

3.   Kéuih dá dihn-wá béi gūng-sī ge tùhng-sih.
　　佢 打 電 話 畀 公 司 嘅 同 事 。

4.   Néih pàhng-yáuh dá dihn-wá béi néih.
　　你 朋 友 打 電 話 畀 你 。

5. Kéuih dá dihn-wá béi bīn-go a?

　佢　打　電　話　畀　邊　個　呀　？

6. Ngóh dá dihn-wá béi taai-táai.

　我　打　電　話　畀　太　太　。

PYRAMID DRILLS   *(CD 1, Track 27)*

1.
chìh-dī

遲　啲

chìh-dī dá-làih

遲　啲　打　嚟

Chéng néih chìh-dī dá-làih lā.

請　你　遲　啲　打　嚟　啦　。

2.
dá dihn-wá

打　電　話

dá dihn-wá béi ngóh

打　電　話　畀　我

kéuih dá dihn-wá béi ngóh

佢　打　電　話　畀　我

giu kéuih dá dihn-wá béi ngóh

叫　佢　打　電　話　畀　我

néih giu kéuih dá dihn-wá béi ngóh

你　叫　佢　打　電　話　畀　我

M̀h-gòi néih giu kéuih dá dihn-wá béi ngóh lā.

唔　該　你　叫　佢　打　電　話　畀　我　啦　。

3.   géi-dō houh dihn-wá
           幾　多　號　電　話
       Kéuih géi-dō houh dihn-wá a?
       佢　幾　多　號　電　話　呀 ？
   Kéuih pàhng-yáuh géi-dō houh dihn-wá a?
   佢　朋　友　幾　多　號　電　話　呀 ？

4.   dá dihn-wá
             打　電　話
       dá dihn-wá béi Chàhn sìn-sàang
       打　電　話　畀　陳　先　生
   Bīn-go dá dihn-wá béi Chàhn sìn-sàang a?
   邊　個　打　電　話　畀　陳　先　生　呀 ？

SUBSTITUTION DRILLS   *(CD 1, Track 28)*

1. Wòhng táai dá dihn-wá béi néih. 黃太打電話畀你。

    a) Chàhn síu-jé 陳小姐   *b)* Néih tùhng-sih 你同事
    c) Kéuih 佢   *d)* Néih pàhng-yáuh 你朋友

2. Néih dihn-wá géi-dō houh a? 你電話幾多號呀？

    a) Chàhn táai 陳太   *b)* Kéuih gūng-sī 佢公司
    c) Néih ūk-kéi 你屋企   *d)* Wòhng sàang ūk-kéi 黃生屋企

GUIDED CONVERSATION

Two students pretend to meet for the first time, they exchange their business cards and ask each other's phone number.

REVIEW EXERCISE

Translation

1. My office phone number is 2397 0428.

2. He called Mrs Chan.

3. Is your home number 3627 5600.

4. Who called me?

5. Sorry, please call later.

LISTENING EXERCISE   *(CD 1, Track 29)*

Listen to the dialogues and choose the correct answer

1. _____   2. _____   3. _____   4. _____

5. _____   6. _____   7. _____

Lesson 6

How Much Is This?

CONVERSATION *(CD 1, Track 30)*

 Mh-gòi, ngóh séung tái-háh nī-go.
唔 該 ， 我 想 睇 吓 呢 個 。
Excuse me, I want to have a look at this one.

 Hóu a. Néih yiu māt-yéh sīk ga?
好 呀 。 你 要 乜 嘢 色 㗎 ？
Yes. What colour do you want?

 Ngóh yiu hùhng-sīk. Yáuh móuh daaih-dī ga?
我 要 紅 色 。 有 冇 大 啲 㗎 ？
I want a red one. Do you have a bigger one?

 Yáuh, chéng néih dáng dáng.
有 ， 請 你 等 等 。
Yes, just a moment please.

 Géi-dō chín a?.
幾 多 錢 呀 ？
How much is this?

 Gáu sahp luhk mān, chāt ńgh jit, jīk-haih chāt sahp yih mān.
九 十 六 蚊 ， 七 五 折 ， 即 係 七 十 二 蚊 。
$96, 25% off, that is $72.

Pèhng-dī lā.   Chāt sahp mān dāk lā.
平 啲 啦 。 七 十 蚊 得 啦 。
Cheaper please, $70, O.K.?

Hóu lā.   Dò-jeh saai.
好 啦 。 多 謝 晒 。
Alright. Thank you very much.

VOCABULARY   *(CD 1, Track 31)*

1. yáuh 有   V : have; possess; exist

2. móuh 冇   V : do not have;
                            without

> 'móuh 冇' is the oppsite of 'yáuh 有'. Don't say 'm̀h-yáuh'.

3. chín 錢   N : money
    eg. Géi(-dō) chín a? 幾(多)錢呀？ : How much is this?

4. jit 折   N : discount
    eg. gáu jit 九折 : 10% off
        chāt ńgh jit 七五折 : 25% off
        Géi-dō jit? 幾多折 : How much discount?

5. dāk 得   ADJ : OK

6. hóu 好   ADJ : fine; good
                     ADV : very

7. daaih 大   ADJ : big; large

8. sai 細   ADJ : small

9. gwai 貴   ADJ : expensive

10. pèhng 平   ADJ : cheap

11. leng 靚   ADJ : beautiful, good looking; good quality

12. sàn 新 ADJ : new

13. dī 啲 ADV : a little more

SENTENCE PATTERNS (CD 1, Track 32)

A. Money

Cents and dollars

10 cents	yāt hòuh(-jí) 一毫（子）
20 cents	léuhng hòuh(-jí) 兩毫（子）
50 cents	ńgh hòuh(-jí) 五毫（子）
$1	yāt mān 一蚊
$2	léuhng mān 兩蚊
$10	sahp mān 十蚊

Cents and dollars combined

$1.20	go-yih 個二
$1.50	go-bun 個半
$7.50	chāt-go-bun 七個半
$2.20	léuhng-go-yih 兩個二
$2.40	léuhng-go-sei 兩個四
$6.90	luhk-go-gáu 六個九
$10.10	sahp-go-lìhng-yāt 十個零一
$20.50	yih-sahp-go-lìhng-ńgh 二十個零五
$24.80	yah-sei-go-baat 廿四個八
$40.20	sei-sahp-go-lìhng-yih 四十個零二

PRACTICE

I.   Read the following money terms

1. $26.70	5. $10.70	9. $0.50	13. $2.20
2. $65.20	6. $13.90	10. $23.20	14. $91.40
3. $99.80	7. $49.40	11. $89.10	15. $54.60
4. $58.30	8. $72.00	12. $0.80	

II.   Listen and write down the amount of money

1. _____   2. _____   3. _____   4. _____

5. _____   6. _____   7. _____   8. _____

9. _____   10. _____

B.   Possession and existence : 'yáuh' 有   *(CD 1, Track 33)*

☞   *Affirmative statement :*   yáuh + noun
有 + 名詞

eg. Yáuh jit.
有 折 。 (There is a discount.)

☞   *Negative statement :*   móuh + noun
冇 + 名詞

eg. Móuh jit.
冇 折 。 (There is no discount.)

☞   *Question form :*   yáuh móuh + noun + a?
有冇 + 名詞 + 呀 ?

eg. Yáuh móuh jit a?

　　有　冇　折　呀　? (Is there any discount?)

Answer: Yáuh. / Móuh.

　　　　有。/ 冇。　　(Yes. / No.)

1. Ngóh yáuh kéuih gūng-sī dihn-wá.
   我　有　佢　公　司　電　話。

2. Néih yáuh móuh sàam sahp mān a?
   你　有　冇　三　十　蚊　呀　?

3. Yáuh móuh daaih-dī ga?
   有　冇　大　啲　㗎　?

4. Nī-go yáuh géi-dō jit a?
   呢　個　有　幾　多　折　呀　?

5. Kéuih móuh pàhng-yáuh.
   佢　冇　朋　友。

6. Chàhn sàang yáuh kāat-pín.
   陳　生　有　卡　片。

C.　A little more : 'dī' 啲　*(CD 1, Track 34)*

☞　Adjective + dī
　　形容詞 + 啲

　　eg. gwai-dī
　　　貴　啲。　(a little more expensive)

1. Yáuh móuh hóu-dī ga?
   有　冇　好　啲　㗎　?

2. Yáuh móuh sai-dī ga?
   有　冇　細　啲　㗎 ？

3. Yáuh móuh pèhng-dī ga?
   有　冇　平　啲　㗎 ？

4. Nī-go sàn-dī.
   呢　個　新　啲 。

5. Ngóh ge pàhng-yáuh leng-dī.
   我　嘅　朋　友　靚　啲 。

6. Kéuih ūk-kéi daaih-dī.
   佢　屋　企　大　啲 。

7. Bīn-go gwai-dī a?
   邊　個　貴　啲　呀 ？

D. Colours (CD 1, Track 35)

1. hāk-sīk 黑色   black
2. baahk-sīk 白色   white
3. hùhng-sīk 紅色   red
4. wòhng-sīk 黃色   yellow
5. làahm-sīk 藍色   blue
6. luhk-sīk 綠色   green
7. cháang-sīk 橙色   orange colour
8. jí-sīk 紫色   purple
9. (ga-)fē-sīk（咖）啡色   brown
10. fán-hùhng-sīk 粉紅色   pink
11. fùi-sīk 灰色   grey
12. gàm-sīk 金色   gold
13. ngàhn-sīk 銀色   silver

PRACTICE

What colour is this? :   Māt-yéh sīk a?

　　　　　　　　　　乜　嘢　色　呀？

PYRAMID DRILLS   *(CD 1, Track 36)*

1.
　　　　　　　　hāk-sīk
　　　　　　　　黑　色
　　　　　　yáuh hāk-sīk
　　　　　　有　黑　色
　　　　Nī-go yáuh hāk-sīk
　　　　呢　個　有　黑　色
　　Nī-go yáuh móuh hāk-sīk ga?
　　呢　個　有　冇　黑　色　㗎？

2.   sai-dī
                            細　啲
                        móuh sai-dī
                       冇　細　啲
                   yáuh móuh sai-dī ga?
                  有　冇　細　啲　㗎？
             Hùhng-sīk ge yáuh móuh sai-dī ga?
            紅　色　嘅　有　冇　細　啲　㗎？

SUBSTITUTION DRILLS   *(CD 1, Track 37)*

1. Yáuh móuh daaih-dī ga? 有冇大啲㗎？

    a) sai 細   *b)* pèhng 平
    c) leng 靚   *d)* gwai 貴

2. Yáuh móuh kāat-pín a? 有冇卡片呀？

    a) dihn-wá 電話   *b)* pàhng-yáuh 朋友
    c) jit 折   *d)* luhk-sīk 綠色

REVIEW EXERCISE

Translation

1. Do you have a blue one?

2. Cheaper, please. How about $50?

3. This one does not come in orange.

4. What colour is this?

5.   The yellow one (costs) $75, the red one (costs) $38.

6.   Does the pink one comes in a larger size?

7.   Which one is newer?

LISTENING EXERCISE   *(CD 1, Track 38)*

I.   **Listen to the following. If the English matches the Cantonese, write down Y, if not, write N.**

1. _____   2. _____   3. _____

4. _____   5. _____   6. _____

II.   **Listen to the dialogues and choose the correct answer.**

1. _____   2. _____   3. _____

4. _____   5. _____   6. _____

Lesson 7

What Time Is It?

Néih géi dím fàan-gùng ga?
你 幾 點 返 工 㗎 ？
What time do you go to work?

> 'géi dím' is a short form of 'gei-dō dím'.

Ngóh gáu-dím fàan-gùng.
我 九 點 返 工 。
I go to work at 9:00.

Néih géi-dō dím sihk aan a?
你 幾 多 點 食 晏 呀 ？
What time do you have lunch?

Ngóh sahp-yih-dím-bun sihk aan.
我 十 二 點 半 食 晏 。
I have lunch at 12:30.

Néih géi dím fàan ūk-kéi a?
你 幾 點 返 屋 企 呀 ？
What time do you go home?

Ngóh luhk-dím-sàam fàan ūk-kéi.
我 六 點 三 返 屋 企 。
I go home at 6:15.

VOCABULARY   *(CD 1, Track 40)*

1.	fàan ūk-kéi 返屋企	VO :	go home
2.	fàan-gūng 返工	VO :	go to work
3.	sihk-faahn 食飯	VO :	eat a meal
4.	sihk jóu-chāan 食早餐	VO :	eat breakfast
5.	sihk aan 食晏	VO :	eat lunch
6.	sihk máahn-faahn 食晚飯	VO :	eat dinner
7.	fan-gaau 瞓覺	VO :	sleep
8.	jouh 做	VO :	to do

eg. jouh māt-yéh? 做乜嘢 : What are you doing?

9. géi(-dō) dím 幾（多）點   QW : what time

SENTENCE PATTERNS   *(CD 1, Track 41)*

A. Telling Clock Time

12:00   sahp-yih-dím (-jūng)
十二點(鐘)

2:05   léuhng-dím-yāt
二點一

9:10   gáu-dím-yih
九點二

4:15   sei-dím-sàam
四點三

6:20   luhk-dím-sei
        六點四

3:25   sàam-dím-nǵh
        三點五

10:30   sahp-dím-bun
        十點半

5:35   nǵh-dím-chāt
        五點七

7:40   chāt-dím-baat
        七點八

11:45   sahp-yāt-dím-gáu
        十一點九

4:50   sei-dím-sahp
        四點十

1:55   yāt-dím-sahp-yāt
        一點十一

PRACTICE

I. Translate the time into English

1. sei-dím-gáu 四點九
2. sahp-yih-dím-sàam 十二點三
3. ńgh-dím-bun 五點半
4. léuhng-dím-sahp 兩點十
5. baat-dím-chāt 八點七

II. Tell the time in Cantonese

1. 5:25	6. 11:10	11. 8:14
2. 9:15	7. 3:59	12. 6:04
3. 1:20	8. 2:39	13. 10:40
4. 7:16	9. 12:45	14. 5:47
5. 6:35	10. 4:30	15. 11:55

B. Subject + time + verb   *(CD 1, Track 42)*

☞ Subject + point of time + verb
   主語 ＋ 時間詞 ＋ 動詞

   eg. Kéuih baat-dím fàan-gùng.
   佢 八 點 返 工 。
   (He goes to work at 8:00.)

☞ Subject + gei(-dō) dím + verb + a?
   主語 ＋ 幾（多）點 ＋ 動詞 ＋ 呀 ？

   eg. Néih géi(-dō) dím fàan-gùng a?
   你 幾 （多） 點 返 工 呀 ？
   (What time do/will you go to work?)

☞ Subject + gei(-dō) dím + verb + ga?

主語 + 幾（多）點 + 動詞 + 㗎？

eg. Néih géi(-dō) dím fàan-gùng ga?

你 幾 （多） 點 返 工 㗎？

(What time do/did you go to work?)

☞ Subject + point of time + jouh māt-yéh a?

主語 + 時間詞 + 做乜嘢呀？

eg. Néih ńgh dím jouh māt-yéh a?

你 五 點 做 乜 嘢 呀？

(What do you do at 5:00?)

1. Ngóh sàam-dím-bun fàan ūk-kéi.

   我 三 點 半 返 屋 企。

2. Kéuih taai-táai gáu-dím-sàam fàan-gùng.

   佢 太 太 九 點 三 返 工。

3. Néih luhk-dím jouh māt-yéh a?

   你 六 點 做 乜 嘢 呀？

4. Ngóh tùhng-sih ńgh-dím-bun fàan ūk-kéi.

   我 同 事 五 點 半 返 屋 企。

5. Néih pàhng-yáuh géi dím sihk jóu-chāan a?

   你 朋 友 幾 點 食 早 餐？

6. Ngóh sahp-yāt-dím fan-gaau.

   我 十 一 點 瞓 覺。

7. Kéuih gūng-sī géi dím sihk aan ga?

   佢 公 司 幾 點 食 晏 㗎？

8. Kéuih ūk-kéi chāt-dím-gáu sihk máahn-faahn.

   佢 屋 企 七 點 九 食 晚 飯。

9. Kéuih baat-dím-bun jouh māt-yéh a?

　　佢　八　點　半　做　乜　嘢　呀　?

10. Kéuih gei-dō dím sihk faahn a?

　　佢　幾　多　點　食　飯　呀　?

PRACTICE

Use two pens as hands of the clock, ask each other what time is it,
and what each other is doing at that time.

What time is it? :   Géi-dō dím a?

　　　　　　　　　　幾　多　點　呀　?

What are you doing? : Neih jouh māt-yéh a?

　　　　　　　　　　你　做　乜　嘢　呀　?

PYRAMID DRILLS   *(CD 1, Track 43)*

fàan-gùng

返 工

baat-dím-bun fàan-gùng

八 點 半 返 工

Kéuih baat-dím-bun fàan-gùng.

佢 八 點 半 返 工 。

SUBSTITUTION DRILLS   *(CD 1, Track 44)*

1. Néih gei-dō dím sihk-faahn a? 你幾多點食飯呀？

    a) faàn ūk-kéi 返屋企   *b)* fan-gaau 瞓覺

    c) fàan-gùng 返工   *d)* sihk jóu-chāan 食早餐

2. Kéuih baat-dím faàn ūk-kéi. 佢八點返屋企 。

    a) 9:30   *b)* 7:15   *c)* 3:20   *d)* 5:10

REVIEW EXERCISE

Translation

1. What time will you go home?

2. I have lunch at 1:00.

3. What will your colleague do at 3:30?

4. What time does your friend have breakfast?

5. He slept at 11:45.

LISTENING EXERCISE   *(CD 1, Track 45)*

Use the given information below, listen to the CD and answer the questions.

8:00	breakfast
8:30	go to work
8:30 – 8:50	take MTR
9:00 – 1:00	work
1:00 – 2:00	lunch
2:00 – 6:00	work
6:00 – 6:25	take minibus
6:30	go home
7:30	dinner
11:00	sleep

1. _____ 2. _____

3. _____ 4. _____

5. _____ 6. _____

7. _____ 8. _____

Lesson 8

I Am Busy

(CD 2, Track 1)

A. Asking time

Yih-gā géi dím a?
而 家 幾 點 呀？
What time is it?

Yāt-dím la. Ngóh-deih heui sihk-faahn lā.
一 點 喇 。 我 哋 去 食 飯 啦 。
It's one o'clock. Let's go for lunch.

Hóu a! Ngóh hóu tóuh-ngoh.
好 呀 ！ 我 好 肚 餓 。
Good! I'm hungry.

Néih géi-dím sihk jóu-chāan ga?
你 幾 點 食 早 餐 㗎？
What time did you have breakfast?

Ngóh chāt-dím-bun sihk jóu-chāan.
我 七 點 半 食 早 餐 。
I have breakfast at 7:30.

B. Mr Chan asks Mrs Wong what time he will leave the office *(CD 2, Track 2)*

Néih géi dím jáu a?

你 幾 點 走 呀 ?

What time will you leave?

Ngóh luhk-dím jáu.

我 六 點 走 。

I'll leave at 6:00.

Ngóh-deih heui sihk-faahn lā.

我 哋 去 食 飯 啦 。

Let's go for dinner.

M̀h-hóu la. Ngóh fàan ūk-kéi tùhng sìn-sàang sihk-faahn.

唔 好 喇 。 我 返 屋 企 同 先 生 食 飯 。

That's not a good idea. I'll go home to have dinner with my husband.

C. Mrs Ho asks Mr Wong why he is so tired *(CD 2, Track 3)*

Hóu gwuih a!

好 攰 呀 !

I'm very tired!

Néih kàhm-máahn géi dím fan-gaau ga?

你 琴 晚 幾 點 瞓 覺 㗎 ?

What time did you sleep last night?

Ngóh kàhm-máahn léuhng-dím fan-gaau.

我 琴 晚 兩 點 瞓 覺 。

I slept at 2:00 last night.

Dím-gáai a?

點 解 呀 ？

Why?

Yàn-waih ngóh tái dihn-sih.

因 爲 我 睇 電 視 。

It's because I watched TV.

READING   *(CD 2, Track 4)*

Ngóh chāt-dím-bun sihk jóu-chāan, baat-dím daap-chè fàan-gùng.

我 七 點 牛 食 早 餐 ， 八 點 搭 車 返 工 。

I have breakfast at 7:30, take a bus to work at 8:00.

Ngóh yāt-dím tùhng tùhng-sih sihk aan. Ngóh luhk-dím fàan ūk-

我 一 點 同 同 事 食 晏 。 我 六 點 返 屋

I have lunch with colleagues at 1:00. I go home at 6:00,

kéi, yìhn-hauh tùhng taai-táai sihk-faahn. Sihk-faahn jì-hauh,

企 ， 然 後 同 太 太 食 飯 。 食 飯 之 後 ，

and then have dinner with my wife. After dinner,

ngóh tái dihn-sih. Ngóh sahp-yāt-dím fan-gaau.

我 睇 電 視 。 我 十 一 點 瞓 覺 。

I watch TV. I sleep at 11:00.

VOCABULARY   *(CD 2, Track 5)*

1. làih or lèih 嚟   V : come

2. heui 去   V : go

3. daap-chè 搭車   VO : take a transport

4. tái dihn-sih 睇電視   VO : watch TV

5. tùhng(-màaih) 同（埋）   CON : and; together with

6. yìh-gā 而家   TW : now

7. géi 幾 + ADJ   ADV : quite

8. tóuh-ngoh 肚餓   ADJ : hungry

9. báau 飽   ADJ : full (stomach)

10. háu-hot 口渴   ADJ : thirsty

11. gwuih 劮 / 癝   ADJ : tired

12. ngáahn-fan 眼瞓   ADJ : sleepy

13. mòhng 忙   ADJ : busy

14. dāk-hàahn 得閒   ADJ : have free time

SENTENCE PATTERNS   *(CD 2, Track 6)*

A. Purpose

☞ action 1 + action 2 (purpose of action 1) + action
3 (purpose of action 2)
動作 1 ＋ 動作 2（動作 1 的目的）＋ 動作 3
（動作 2 的目的）

eg. Ngóh-deih daap-chè heui sihk-faahn.
我 哋 搭 車 去 食 飯 。
(We take public transport to go eat.)

1. Ngóh fàan ūk-kéi tái dihn-sih.
我 返 屋 企 睇 電 視 。

2. Ngóh-deih heui sihk jóu-chāan lā.
   我 哋 去 食 早 餐 啦 。

3. Ngóh daap síu-bā fàan-gùng.
   我 搭 小 巴 返 工 。

4. Néih-deih làih ngóh ūk-kéi sihk-faahn lā.
   你 哋 嚟 我 屋 企 食 飯 啦 。

5. Chàhn sàang daap-chè fàan ūk-kéi.
   陳 生 搭 車 返 屋 企 。

6. Néih heui kéuih gūng-sī jouh māt-yéh a?
   你 去 佢 公 司 做 乜 嘢 呀 ？

B. And/with : 'tùhng' 同 *(CD 2, Track 7)*

Affirmative statement :

☞ noun 1 + tùhng + noun 2
   名詞 1 + 同 + 名詞 2

   eg. Ngóh tùhng taai-táai sihk-faahn.
   我 同 太 太 食 飯 。
   (I eat with my wife.)

Negative statement :

☞ noun 1 + m̀h-tùhng + noun 2
   名詞 1 + 唔同 + 名詞 2

   eg. Ngóh m̀h-tùhng taai-táai sihk-faahn.
   我 唔 同 太 太 食 飯 。
   (I don't eat with my wife.)

Question form :

☞ noun 1 + tùhng m̀h-tùhng + noun 2 + a?
    名詞 1 + 同 唔 同 + 名詞 2 + 呀 ？

   eg. Néih tùhng m̀h-tùhng taai-táai sihk-faahn a?
        你 同 唔 同 太 太 食 飯 呀 ？
        (Do you eat with your wife?)

        Answer: Tùhng. / M̀h-tùhng.
                  同 。/ 唔 同 。   (Yes./No.)

☞ Person A + tùhng(-màaih) + bīn-go + verb + a?
    人 A + 同 (埋) + 邊 個 + 動 詞 + 呀 ？

   eg. Néih tùhng bīn-go sihk-faahn a?
        你 同 邊 個 食 飯 呀 ？
        (Who do you eat with?)

1. Ngóh tùhng pàhng-yáuh sihk jóu-chāan.
   我 同 朋 友 食 早 餐 。

2. Néih tùhng bīn-go làih ngóh ūk-kéi a?
   你 同 邊 個 嚟 我 屋 企 呀 ？

3. Kéuih tùhng taai-táai fàan ūk-kéi.
   佢 同 太 太 返 屋 企 。

4. Ngóh tùhng tùhng-sih yāt-dím sihk aan.
   我 同 同 事 一 點 食 晏 。

5. Néih sìn-sàang tùhng-m̀h-tùhng néih sihk-faahn a?
   你 先 生 同 唔 同 你 食 飯 呀 ？

6. Néih tùhng-m̀h-tùhng ngóh heui a?
   你 同 唔 同 我 去 呀 ？

7. Ngóh m̀h-tùhng kéuih daap dīk-sí.
    我 唔 同 佢 搭 的 士 。

8. Ngóh m̀h-tùhng kéuih fàan ūk-kéi.
    我 唔 同 佢 返 屋 企 。

C. Use of adjectives   *(CD 2, Track 8)*

☞ *high degree* : hóu mòhng
                    好 忙   (very busy)
                    géi mòhng
                    幾 忙   (quite busy)
☞ *medium* :   m̀h-haih géi mòhng
                    唔 係 幾 忙   (not very busy)
☞ *low degree* : m̀h-mòhng
                    唔 忙   (not busy)

1. Kéuih hóu háu-hot.
    佢 好 口 渴 。

2. Ngóh pàhng-yáuh ge ūk-kéi géi daaih.
    我 朋 友 嘅 屋 企 幾 大 。

3. Wòhng sàang ge taai-táai hóu hóu.
    黃 生 嘅 太 太 好 好 。

4. Chàhn síu-jé géi báau.
    陳 小 姐 幾 飽 。

5. Kéuih-deih m̀h-dāk-hàahn.
    佢 哋 唔 得 閒 。

6. Kéuih ge pàhng-yáuh leng m̀h-leng a?
    佢 嘅 朋 友 靚 唔 靚 呀 ?

7. Ngóh hóu mòhng, m̀h-tùhng néih sihk-faahn la.
   我 好 忙 ， 唔 同 你 食 飯 喇 。

8. Néih tóuh m̀h-tóuh-ngoh a?
   你 肚 唔 肚 餓 呀 ？

9. Ngóh m̀h-haih géi gwuih.
   我 唔 係 幾 劫 。

10. Ngóh hóu ngáahn-fan.
    我 好 眼 瞓 。

REVIEW FINAL PARTICLES

a 呀 :	exclamation; choice type question; question with question word(s)
ga 㗎 :	ge + a 嘅 + 呀; asking habits; asking when action(s) has been completed; exclamation
lā / ā 啦 / 吖 :	please; let's; listing examples
la 喇 :	indicating changes; already
àh 吖 :	I suppose?

1. Yāt dím _____ . Yāt-chàih (*together) heui sihk aan _____ .
   一 點 _____ 。 一 齊 去 食 晏 _____ 。

2. Ngóh-deih heui sihk-faahn, néih m̀h-heui _____ ?
   我 哋 去 食 飯 ， 你 唔 去 _____ ？

3. Ngóh hóu tóuh-ngóh. Heui sihk-faahn _____ .
   我 好 肚 餓 。 去 食 飯 _____ 。

4. Néih géi dím sihk jóu-chāan ____?

   你 幾 點 食 早 餐 ____?

5. Ngóh-deih géi dím sihk-faahn ____?

   我 哋 幾 點 食 飯 ____?

6. Ngóh yìh-gā fàan ūk-kéi ____.

   我 而 家 返 屋 企 ____。

7. Ngóh-deih yāt-chàih (*together) daap-chè jáu ____.

   我 哋 一 齊 搭 車 走 ____。

8. Néih kàhm-máahn (*last night) géi dím fan-gaau ____?

   你 琴 晚 幾 點 瞓 覺 ____?

PYRAMID DRILLS   *(CD 2, Track 9)*

1.   sihk-faahn

             食 飯

          fàan ūk-kéi sihk-faahn

          返 屋 企 食 飯

       daap síu-bā fàan ūk-kéi sihk-faahn

       搭 小 巴 返 屋 企 食 飯

    Ngóh daap síu-bā fàan ūk-kéi sihk-faahn

    我 搭 小 巴 返 屋 企 食 飯

2.   Néih heui

              你 去

          Néih tùhng taai-táai heui

          你 同 太 太 去

Néih m̀h-tùhng taai-táai heui
你　唔　同　太　太　去
Néih tùhng m̀h-tùhng taai-táai heui a?
你　同　唔　同　太　太　去　呀？

SUBSTITUTION DRILLS   *(CD 2, Track 10)*

1. Ngóh tùhng <u>pàhng-yáuh</u> sihk-faahn. 我同朋友食飯。

   a) tùhng-sih 同事　　　　　　*b)* taai-táai 太太

   c) Chàhn sàang 陳生　　　　*d)* Wòhng síu-jé 黃小姐

2. Kéuih hóu <u>tóuh-ngoh</u>. 佢好肚餓。

   a) gwuih 边　　　　　　　　*b)* dāk-hàahn 得閒

   c) `ngáahn-fan 眼瞓　　　　*d)* mòhng 忙

REVIEW EXERCISE

I.　Rewrite the following sentences

   1. faàn ūk-kéi / ngóh / ńgh-dím / daap dīk-sí
      返 屋 企 ／ 我 ／ 五 點 ／ 搭 的 士

   2. kéuih-deih / sihk-faahn / yāt-dím
      佢 哋 ／ 食 飯 ／ 一 點

   3. taai-táai / m̀h-tùhng / kéuih / sihk-faahn
      太 太 ／ 唔 同 ／ 佢 ／ 食 飯

   4. hóu / dāk-hàahn / ngóh / pàhng-yáuh
      好 ／ 得 閒 ／ 我 ／ 朋 友

II. Fill in the blanks

1. Ngóh baat-dím-bun (a.m.) _____ .

    我　八　點　半 _____ 。

2. Ngóh sahp-yih-dím _____ .

    我　十　二　點 _____ 。

3. Ngóh tùhng _____ sihk-faahn.

    我　同 _____ 食　飯 。

4. Néih _____ tùhng-sih sihk-faahn a?

    你 _____ 同　事　食　飯　呀 ?

5. Kéuih _____ taai-táai _____ .

    佢 _____ 太　太 _____ 。

III. Translation

1. I go to work by bus at 8:30.

2. They came at 7:15, (and then) went home at 10:30.

3. I will not have lunch with my wife.

4. I am not busy.

5. He feels sleepy.

6. Who do you have dinner with?

7. I'm going home now.

8. I am watching TV with my friends.

IV. Ask and answer the questions

1. (gwai 貴)

Bīn-gihn gwai-dī a?

邊 件 貴 啲 呀 ?

2. (daaih 大)

Bīn-go daaih-dī a?

邊 個 大 啲 呀 ?

3. (pèhng 平)

Bīn-go pèhng-dī a?

邊 個 平 啲 呀 ?

4. (sàn 新)

Bīn-go sàn-dī a?
邊 個 新 啲 呀 ？

5. (leng 靚)

Bīn-go leng-dī a?
邊 個 靚 啲 呀 ？

6. (mòhng 忙)

Bīn-go mòhng-dī a?
邊 個 忙 啲 呀 ？

7. (gwuih 趷)

Bīn-go gwuih-dī a?
邊　個　趷　啲　呀？

8. (sai 細)

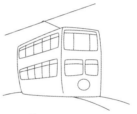

Māt-yéh chè sai-dī a?
乜　嘢　車　細　啲　呀？

LISTENING EXERCISE   *(CD 2, Track 11)*

I. Multiple choice

1. It's now 7:30   _____

2. He and his colleague   _____

3. I go for lunch at 1:00   _____

4. Go home by car   _____

II.   Listen to the dialogues and choose the correct answer.

1. _____   2. _____   3. _____

4. _____   5. _____   6. _____

III.   Use the given information and answer the questions.

7:10	have breakfast
8:00	take a taxi to work (with my wife)
9:00	start working
12:30	have lunch (with colleagues)
8:20	have dinner (with friends)
9:45	go home
11:15	sleep

1.   Néih géi dím sihk jóu-chāan a?
     你 幾 點 食 早 餐 呀 ？

2.   Néih géi dím fan-gaau a?
     你 幾 點 瞓 覺 呀 ？

3.   Néih tùhng bīn-go sihk aan a?
     你 同 邊 個 食 晏 呀 ？

4.   Néih tùhng taai-táai sihk-faahn, haih m̀h-haih a?
     你 同 太 太 食 飯 ， 係 唔 係 呀 ？

5.   Néih gáu-dím-bun fàan ūk-kéi, haih m̀h-haih a?
     你 九 點 半 返 屋 企 ， 係 唔 係 呀 ？

6.   Néih daap síu-bā fàan-gùng, haih m̀h-haih a?
     你 搭 小 巴 返 工 ， 係 唔 係 呀 ？

Lesson 9

In A Hong Kong Style Cafe

Sìn-sàang yiu dī māt-yéh a?
先 生 要 啲 乜 嘢 呀？
What do you want?/What would you like?

Yáuh móuh chà-sìu faahn a?
有 冇 叉 燒 飯 呀？
Do you have BBQ pork with rice?

Yáuh.
有 。
Yes.

Yiu wún chà-sìu faahn lā.
要 碗 叉 燒 飯 啦 。
A bowl of BBQ pork with rice please.

'Yiu wún' is a short form of 'Yiu yāt wún 要一碗'.

Yiu dī mè yám a?
要 啲 咩 飲 呀 ？
Do you want anything to drink?

'mè' = 'māt-yéh'
'咩' = '乜嘢'

Béi bùi ga-fē ngóh lā, m̀h-gòi.
畀 杯 咖 啡 我 啦，唔 該 。
Please give me a cup of coffee.

Yiht dihng dung a?
熱 定 凍 呀 ？
Hot or cold?

Yiht ge.
熱 嘅 。
Hot.

*   *   *   *   *   *

Ṁh-gòi néih béi go B chāan ngóh nìng-jáu, yám dung náaih-chàh.
唔 該 你 畀 個 B 餐 我 擰 走 ，飲 凍 奶 茶 。
Please give me a set B, take away, the drink is iced tea with milk.

Hóu aak. Chéng néih dáng dáng.
好 呃 。 請 你 等 等 。
Yes. Please wait a moment.

VOCABULARY   *(CD 2, Track 13)*

1. yiht 熱   ADJ : hot

2. dung 凍   ADJ : cold

3. nìhng-mūng-chàh or
    lìhng-mūng-chàh 檸檬茶   N : lemon tea

4. náaih-chàh or láaih-chàh 奶茶 N : tea with milk

5. ga-fē 咖啡   N : coffee

6. hó-lohk 可樂   N : coke

7. chà-sìu faahn 叉燒飯   N : BBQ pork with rice

8. wún 碗   N : bowl

9. bùi 杯   N : cup, glass, mug

10. yiu 要   V/AV : want; need

11. yám 飲   V : drink

12. béi 畀   V : give

13. nìng-jáu or lìng-jáu 擰走   V : take away, carry out

14. hái douh sihk 喺度食   PH : eat here

SENTENCE PATTERNS   *(CD 2, Track 14)*

Give : 'béi' 畀

☞ Person A + béi + measure + object + Person B

   人 A + 畀 + 量詞 + 名詞 + 人 B

   eg. Kéuih béi bùi chàh ngóh.

   佢　畀　杯　茶　我　。

   (He gives me a cup of tea.)

1. M̀h-gòi néih béi bùi ga-fē ngóh lā.

    唔　該　你　畀　杯　咖　啡　我　啦　。

2. M̀h-gòi néih béi bùi chàh kéuih lā.

    唔　該　你　畀　杯　茶　佢　啦　。

3. M̀h-gòi béi wún chà-sìu faahn.
    唔 該 畀 碗 叉 燒 飯 。

4. Bīn-go béi sahp mān néih a?
    邊 個 畀 十 蚊 你 呀 ？

5. Néih béi dī māt-yéh Wòhng síu-jé a?
    你 畀 啲 乜 嘢 黃 小 姐 呀 ？

6. Hòh táai béi bùi ga-fē bīn-go a?
    何 太 畀 杯 咖 啡 邊 個 呀 ？

REVIEW EXERCISE

I. Translate the following terms for drinks

1. large coke
2. hot coffee
3. iced tea with milk
4. hot lemon tea
5. iced coffee
6. iced lemon tea

II. Make up dialogues for the following orders

1. 3 hot coffee and 1 iced lemon tea, $14

2. 2 teas with milk, $12

3. 1 coffee take away, $7.50

4. 1 small coke and 1 hot lemon tea, $18.50

5. 1 BBQ pork with rice, eat here, $30

6. 3 orange juice, $30

(CD 2, Track 15)

McDONALD'S MENU Mahk-dòng-lòuh 麥當勞	
hon-bóu-bāau 漢堡包	Hamburger
jī-sí hon-bóu 芝士漢堡	Cheese burger
jyù-láuh dáan hon-bóu 豬柳蛋漢堡	Sausage Mcmuffin w. egg
yīn-yuhk dáan hon-bóu 煙肉蛋漢堡	Egg Mcmuffin
geuih-mòuh-ba 巨無霸	Big Mac
yùh-láuh-bāau 魚柳包	Fillet o'fish
mahk-hèung-gài 麥香雞	MaChicken
mahk-lohk-gài 麥樂雞	McNuggets
syùh-tíu 薯條	French fries
syùh-béng 薯餅	Hash brown
pìhng-gwó pāi 蘋果批	Apple pie
jyū-gwū-līk sàn-déi 朱古力新地	Chocolate sundae
sih-dō-bē-léi sàn-déi 士多啤梨新地	Strawberry sundae
sàn-déi túng 新地筒	Twist cone
syut-bīk 雪碧	Sprite
cháang-jāp 橙汁	Orange juice

Lesson 10
Eating Chinese Dim Sum

A. At the reception

Sìn-sàang, géi wái a?
先 生 ， 幾 位 呀 ？
Sir, how many person?

Sei wái.
四 位 。
Four.

Gwai sing a?
貴 姓 呀 ？
May I know your name?

Ngóh sing Wòhng.
我 姓 黃 。
My name is Wong.

(She gives Mr Wong a number card.)

Chéng dáng jahn.
請 等 陣 。
Please wait a moment.

(Ten minutes later)

45-houh Wòhng sàang, sei wái. M̀h-gòi nī-bihn.
45 號 黃 生 ， 四 位 。 唔 該 呢 邊 。
Number 45 Mr Wong. This way please.

B. At the table *(CD 2, Track 17)*

Géi wái, yám mè chàh a?
幾 位 ， 飲 咩 茶 呀 ？
What kind of tea do you drink?

> géi wái 幾位 : a polite way for a waiter to address a group of people.

Yāt wùh bóu-léi,
yāt wùh gwán séui, m̀h-gòi.
一 壺 普 洱 ，
一 壺 滾 水 ， 唔 該 。
A pot of pu'er tea, a pot of hot water please.

> mè 咩 : a variation of 'māt-yéh 乜嘢' (what)

Séung sihk dī māt-yéh a?
想 食 啲 乜 嘢 呀 ？
What do you want to eat?/What would you like to eat?

Ngóh séung sihk hà-gáau.
我 想 食 蝦 餃 。
I want to eat shrimp dumplings.

Ngóh yiu chèun-gyún.
我 要 春 卷 。
I want spring rolls.

Hòh síu-jé jùng-yi sihk māt-yéh dím-sām a?
何 小 姐 鍾 意 食 乜 嘢 點 心 呀 ？
Miss Ho, what do you like to eat?

Sih-daahn lā.

是 但 啦 。

Up to you.

Sihk m̀h-sihk chà-sìu-bāau a?

食 唔 食 叉 燒 包 呀 ？

Do you like to eat BBQ pork bun?

Hóu aak.

好 呃 。

Yes.

(The dimsum are served on the table.)

Nī-dī haih mè a?

呢 啲 係 咩 呀 ？

What are these?

Nī-dī haih sìu-máai.

呢 啲 係 燒 賣 。

These are pork dumplings.

Hòh síu-jé, néih jùng m̀h-jùng-yi yám chàh a?

何 小 姐 ， 你 鍾 唔 鍾 意 飲 茶 呀 ？

Miss Ho, do you like to eat dim sum?

Ngóh hóu jùng-yi yám chàh. Dī dím-sām hóu hóu-sihk.

我 好 鍾 意 飲 茶 。 啲 點 心 好 好 食 。

I love dim sum. These dim sum are delicious.

Sihk m̀h-sihk faahn a?

食 唔 食 飯 呀 ？

Do you want some rice?

Hóu aak. Yiu yāt-go Yèuhng-jàu cháau-faahn lā.

好 呃 。 要 一 個 揚 州 炒 飯 啦 。

Yes. Let's have a fried rice.

(After a while)

Báau meih a?

飽 未 呀 ？

Are you full?

Géi báau la.

幾 飽 喇 。

I'm quite full.

Ngóh séung sihk sài-máih-louh.

我 想 食 西 米 露 。

I want to have coconut milk with sago.

Ngóh dōu haih.

我 都 係 。

Me too.

(After they finish eating.)

Mh-gòi màaih-dāan.

唔 該 埋 單 。

Bill, please.

Dò-jeh sàam baak mān.

多 謝 三 百 蚊 。

Three hundred dollars please.

Table manner

1. When someone pours tea for you, say 'm̀h-gòi' 唔該 and knock with the first two fingers on the table. This symbolises bowing to show thanks for his/her kindness.

2. When you want to refill the teapot, lift up the lid, put it aside and wait, or you can tell the waiter 'M̀h-gòi chùng séui.' 唔該冲水 or 'M̀h-gòi gà séui' 唔該加水.

3. Use the bowl and spoon for holding food. The plate is for holding bones and left-overs.

READING   *(CD 2, Track 18)*

Gàm-yaht ngóh tùhng dī tùhng-sih heui yám chàh. Ngóh-deih
今   日   我   同   啲   同   事   去   飲   茶 。 我   哋
Today   I   went   for   dim   sum   with   my   colleagues.   We

yám bóu-léi, sihk dím-sām tùhng cháau-faahn. Ngóh-deih
飲   普   洱 ， 食   點   心   同   炒   飯 。 我   哋
drank pu'er tea, ate dim sum and fried rice. We were all

dōu hóu báau. Léuhng dím, ngóh-deih màaih-dāan fàan
都   好   飽 。   兩   點 ， 我   哋   埋   單   返
very full. At two o'clock, we got the bill and went back to

gūng-sī. Hòh síu-jé hóu jùng-yi yám chàh. Ngóh-deih wah
公   司 。   何   小   姐   好   鍾   意   飲   茶 。 我   哋   話
the office. Miss Ho loves dim sum. We said we would go

tìng-yaht dōu heui yám chàh. Kéuih hóu hòi-sàm.
聽 日 都 去 飲 茶 。 佢 好 開 心 。
for dim sum again tomorrow. She was very happy.

Chinese Tea   *(CD 2, Track 19)*

1. bóu-léi/ póu-léi 普洱   Pu'er tea

2. hèung-pín 香片   Jasmine tea

3. tit-gwùn-yàm 鐵觀音   Iron Budha tea

Dim Sum

1. hà-gáau 蝦餃   shrimp dumpling

2. sìu-máai 燒賣   pork dumpling

3. chèun-gyún 春卷   spring roll

4. chà-sìu-chéung 叉燒腸   rice roll with BBQ pork filling

5. hà-chéung 蝦腸   rice roll with shrimp filling

6. wuh-gok 芋   fried mashed taro dumpling

7. chà-sìu-bāau 叉燒包   BBQ pork bun

8. chà-sìu-sōu 叉燒酥   BBQ pork pastry

9. gwun-tòng-gáau 灌湯餃   soup dumpling

10. fuhng-jáau 鳳爪   chicken feet (phoenix claw)

11. pàaih-gwāt 排骨   steamed spare rib

12. jàn-jyū-gāi 珍珠雞   glutinous rice dumpling with
                                chicken filling

13. daahn-tāat 蛋撻   egg tart

14. hùhng-dáu-sā 紅豆沙   red bean sweet soup

15. sài-máih-louh 西米露   coconut milk with sago

16. mòng-gwó bou-dīn 芒果布甸   mango pudding

17. máh-lāai-gōu 馬拉糕   Malaysian sponge cake

Rice and Noodles

1. Yèuhng-jàu cháau-faahn   Fried rice
   揚州炒飯

2. Yūn-yēung faahn 鴛鴦飯   Fried rice with tomato and
                                  cream sauce topping

3. Gòn-sìu yì-mihn 乾燒伊麵(麪)   Fried E-fu noodles with
                                  mushroom

4. Yuhk-sī cháau-mihn   Crunchy noodles with
   肉絲炒麵(麪)   shredded pork

5. Sìng-jàu cháau-máih 星洲炒米   Singapore style fried
                                  vermicelli

6. Gòn-cháau ngàuh hó 乾炒牛河   Fried thick rice noodles
                                  with beef

VOCABULARY   *(CD 2, Track 20)*

1. gàm-yaht 今日   TW : today

2. tìng-yaht 聽日   TW : tomorrow

3. yám 飲   V : drink

4. séui 水   N : water

   eg. gwán-séui 滾水 : boiled water, hot water

      dung-séui 凍水 : cold water

5. dím-sām 點心   N : dim sum

6. faahn 飯   N : rice

   eg. yāt wún faahn 一碗飯 : a bowl of rice

7. máaih 買   V : buy

8. jùng-yi 鍾意   V/AV : like, like to

9. séung 想   AV : want to; wish to

10. hóu sihk 好食   ADJ : delicious; good to eat

11. báau 飽   ADJ : full (stomach)

12. hòi-sàm 開心   ADJ : happy

13. meih 未   ADV : not yet

14. dōu 都   ADV : all, also

SENTENCE PATTERNS   *(CD 2, Track 21)*

A.   Action at present or near future

   Affirmative statement :

   ☞ subject + verb 主詞 + 動詞

     eg. Ngóh yám chàh.

      我 飲 茶 。

      (I drink tea.)

   Negative statement :

   ☞ subject + m̀h + verb 主詞 + 唔 + 動詞

eg. Ngóh m̀h-yám chàh.

我　唔　飲　茶　。

(I don't drink tea.)

Question form :

☞　subject + verb m̀h-verb + (noun +) a?

主詞 + 動詞 唔-動詞 + （名詞 +）呀？

eg. Néih yám m̀h-yám chàh a?

你　飲　唔　飲　茶　呀　？

(Do you drink tea?)

1. Ngóh-deih yám náaih-chàh.

我　哋　飲　奶　茶　。

2. Néih sihk m̀h-sihk dím-sām a?

你　食　唔　食　點　心　呀　？

3. Néih tùhng-sih máaih m̀h-máaih chè a?

你　同　事　買　唔　買　車　呀　？

4. Ngóh jùng-yi ga-fē, m̀h-jùng-yi chàh.

我　鍾　意　咖　啡　，唔　鍾　意　茶　。

5. Néih yám m̀h-yám nìhng-mūng-chàh a?

你　飲　唔　飲　檸　檬　茶　呀　？

6. Kéuih pàhng-yáuh máaih nī-go hùhng-sīk ge.

佢　朋　友　買　呢　個　紅　色　嘅　。

7. Ngóh m̀h-yiu gwán-séui.

我　唔　要　滾　水　。

8. Kéuih-deih yiu sàam wún faahn.

佢　哋　要　三　碗　飯　。

9. Ngóh-deih yìh-gā heui yám chàh. Néih heui m̀h-heui a?

    我 哋 而 家 去 飲 茶 。 你 去 唔 去 呀 ?

10. Néih tái m̀h-tái dihn-sih a?

    你 睇 唔 睇 電 視 呀 ?

B. Like to : 'jùng-yi' 鍾意 *(CD 2, Track 22)*

Affirmative statement :

☞ jùng-yi + verb/noun 鍾意 + 動詞/名詞

  eg. Ngóh jùng-yi yám chàh.
     我 鍾 意 飲 茶 。
     (I like to drink tea.)

     Ngóh jùng-yi chàh.
     我 鍾 意 茶 。
     (I like tea.)

Negative statement :

☞ m̀h-jùng-yi + verb/noun 唔鍾意 + 動詞/名詞

  eg. Ngóh m̀h-jùng-yi yám chàh.
     我 唔 鍾 意 飲 茶 。
     (I don't like to drink tea.)

     Ngóh m̀h-jùng-yi chàh.
     我 唔 鍾 意 茶 。
     (I don't like tea.)

Question form :

☞ jùng m̀h-jùng-yi + verb/noun
   鍾唔鍾意 + 動詞/名詞

eg. Néih jùng m̀h-jùng-yi yám chàh a?

你 鍾 唔 鍾 意 飲 茶 呀 ？

(Do you like to drink tea?)

Néih jùng m̀h-jùng-yi chàh a?

你 鍾 唔 鍾 意 茶 呀 ？

(Do you like tea?)

1. Néih jùng-yi jouh māt-yéh a?

   你 鍾 意 做 乜 嘢 呀 ？

2. Néih-deih jùng m̀h-jùng-yi tái dihn-sih ga?

   你 哋 鍾 唔 鍾 意 睇 電 視 㗎 ？

3. Ngóh jùng-yi sihk-yéh.

   我 鍾 意 食 嘢 。

4. Ngóh m̀h-jùng-yi máaih-yéh.

   我 唔 鍾 意 買 嘢 。

5. Ngóh hóu jùng-yi fan-gaau.

   我 好 鍾 意 瞓 覺 。

6. Ngóh jùng-yi daap syùhn.

   我 鍾 意 搭 船 。

7. Neih jùng-yi māt-yéh dīm-sām a?

   你 鍾 意 乜 嘢 點 心 呀 ？

8. Ngóh m̀h-jùng-yi yám cháang-jāp.

   我 唔 鍾 意 飲 橙 汁 。

9. Néih taai-táai jùng-yi māt-yéh a ?

   你 太 太 鍾 意 乜 嘢 呀 ？

10. Kéuih-deih m̀h-jùng-yi yám séui.

    佢 哋 唔 鍾 意 飲 水 。

C. Want to : 'séung' 想 *(CD 2, Track 23)*

Affirmative statement :

☞ séung + verb 想 ＋ 動詞

   eg. Ngóh séung yám séui.

   我 想 飲 水 。

   (I want to drink water.)

☞ séung yiu + noun 想要 ＋ 名詞

   eg. Ngóh séung yiu yāt bùi séui.

   我 想 要 一 杯 水 。

   (I want a glass of water.)

Negative statement :

☞ m̀h-séung + verb 唔想 ＋ 動詞

   eg. Ngóh m̀h-séung yám séui.

   我 唔 想 飲 水 。

   (I don't want to drink water.)

Question form :

☞ séung m̀h-séung + verb + a? 想唔想 ＋ 動詞 ＋ 呀 ？

   eg. Néih séung m̀h-séung yám séui a?

   你 想 唔 想 飲 水 呀 ？

   (Do you want to drink water?)

1. Kéuih m̀h-yiu chàh, kéuih séung yiu dung séui.

   佢 唔 要 茶 ， 佢 想 要 凍 水 。

2. Kéuih séung máaih nī-dī yéh.

   佢 想 買 呢 啲 嘢 。

3. Kéuih pàhng-yáuh séung yiu hó-lohk.
    佢 朋 友 想 要 可 樂 。

4. Ngóh yìh-gā séung heui sihk-faahn.
    我 而 家 想 去 食 飯 。

5. Ngóh m̀h-séung fàan-gùng, ngóh séung fan-gaau.
    我 唔 想 返 工 ， 我 想 瞓 覺 。

6. Néih séung m̀h-séung tùhng kéuih sihk-faahn a?
    你 想 唔 想 同 佢 食 飯 呀 ？

7. Kéuih m̀h-séung chìh-dou.
    佢 唔 想 遲 到 。

8. Néih séung heui bīn-douh a?
    你 想 去 邊 度 呀 ？

9. Ngóh m̀h-séung hàahng-louh.
    我 唔 想 行 路 。

10. Néih sìng-kèih-yaht séung jouh māt-yéh a?
    你 星 期 日 想 做 乜 嘢 呀 ？

D. Hundreds and Thousands *(CD 2, Track 24)*

100	yāt baak 一百		509	ńgh baak lìhng gáu 五百零九
101	yāt baak lìhng yāt 一百零一		410	sei baak yāt sahp 四百一十
102	yāt baak lìhng yih 一百零二		111	yāt baak yāt sahp yāt 一百一十一
203	yih baak lìhng sàam 二百零三		312	sàam baak yāt sahp yih 三百一十二

604   luhk baak lìhng sei
       六百零四

905   gáu baak lìhng ńgh
       九百零五

306   sàam baak lìhng luhk
       三百零六

807   baat baak lìhng chāt
       八百零七

913   gáu baak yāt sahp sàam
       九百一十三

514   ńgh baak yāt sahp sei
       五百一十四

815   baat baak yāt sahp ńgh
       八百一十五

416   sei baak yāt sahp luhk
       四百一十六

*   *   *   *   *   *

729   chāt baak yih sahp gáu / chāt baak yah gáu
       七百二十九 / 七百廿九

238   yih baak sàam sahp baat / yih baak sà-ah baat
       二百三十八 / 二百卅八

1,000 yāt chìn
       一千

2,001 yih chìn lìhng yāt
       二千零一

3,010 sàam chìn lìhng yāt sahp
       三千零一十

4,567 sei chìn ńgh baak luhk sahp chāt /
       sei chìn ńgh baak luhk-ah chāt
       四千五百六十七

10,000 yāt maahn
       一萬

When numbers are followed by the next digit only:

690   luhk baak gáu (sahp)
       六百九（十）

170   (yāt) baak chāt (sahp)
         (一) 百七 (十)

250   yih baak ńgh (sahp)／léuhng baak ńgh (sahp)
         二 百 五 (十)／兩 百 五 (十)

5,600   ńgh chìn luhk (baak)
         五 千 六 (百)

8,900   baat chìn gáu (baak)
         八 千 九 (百)

34,000   sàam maahn sei (chìn)
         三 萬 四 (千)

PRACTICE

Read the following money terms

1. $107	6. $978	11. $6,989.90	16. $100
2. $110	7. $7,234.50	12. $775.40	17. $545
3. $119.40	8. $615.70	13. $589.10	18. $1,644.30
4. $47,063	9. $406.30	14. $3,575.60	19. $790
5. $666	10. $243.90	15. $198.90	20. $3,080

PYRAMID DRILLS   *(CD 2, Track 25)*

1.   dím-sām
                       點 心
                  sihk dím-sām
                  食 點 心
              Néih sihk dím-sām
              你 食 點 心

Néih m̀h-sihk dím-sām
你　唔　食　點　心
Néih sihk m̀h-sihk dím-sām a?
你　食　唔　食　點　心　呀　？

2.　　　　　　　yám séui
　　　　　　飲　水
　　　　jùng-yi yám séui
　　　鍾　意　飲　水
　　　m̀h-jùng-yi yám séui
　　唔　鍾　意　飲　水
　　Kéuih m̀h-jùng-yi yám séui
　　佢　唔　鍾　意　飲　水
　Kéuih jùng m̀h-jùng-yi yám séui a?
　佢　鍾　唔　鍾　意　飲　水　呀　？

3.　　　　　　hàahng-louh
　　　　　行　路
　　　　hàahng-louh heui
　　　行　路　去
　　séung hàahng-louh heui
　　想　行　路　去
　　m̀h-séung hàahng-louh heui
　唔　想　行　路　去
　Kéuih m̀h-séung hàahng-louh heui
　佢　唔　想　行　路　去
Kéuih séung m̀h-séung hàahng-louh heui a?
佢　想　唔　想　行　路　去　呀　？

SUBSTITUTION DRILLS   *(CD 2, Track 26)*

Ngóh jùng-yi tái dihn-sih.

我 鍾 意 睇 電 視。

a) yám chàh 飲茶   *b)* daap syùhn 搭船

c) sihk chà-sìu-faahn 食叉燒飯 *d)* hàahng-louh 行路

REVIEW EXERCISE

I.   Fill in the blanks

1. Ngóh jùng-yi _____ chàh.

    我 鍾 意 _____ 茶 。

2. Chàhn síu-jé hóu báau. Kéuih _____ sihk-yéh la.

    陳 小 姐 好 飽。 佢 _____ 食 嘢 喇 。

3. Yám _____ séui a?

    飲 _____ 水 呀 ？

4. Néih séung yám _____ chàh a?

    你 想 飲 _____ 茶 呀 ？

5. Hòh sàang _____ hà-gáau a?

    何 生 _____ 蝦 餃 呀 ？

6. Ngóh séung máaih _____ .

    我 想 買 _____ 。

II. Rewrite the following sentences

1. pàhng-yáuh / chè / máaih / kéuih / séung
    朋 友 ／ 車 ／ 買 ／ 佢 ／ 想

2. yám / néih / m̀h / ga-fē / yám / a
    飲 ／ 你 ／ 唔 ／ 咖 啡 ／ 飲 ／ 呀

3. Chàhn / fàan-gùng / jùng-yi / m̀h / sìn-sàang
    陳 ／ 返 工 ／ 鍾 意 ／ 唔 ／ 先 生

4. néih / sihk / bīn-go / faahn / tùhng / séung / a
    你 ／ 食 ／ 邊 個 ／ 飯 ／ 同 ／ 想 ／ 呀

5. séung / māt-yéh / néih / jouh / a / yìh-gā
    想 ／ 乜 嘢 ／ 你 ／ 做 ／ 呀 ／ 而 家

III. Translation

1. What do you want?

2. Four bowls of rice, please.

3. I don't like being late.

4. I want a glass of water.

5. She wants to buy a TV set.

6. Are you going to eat dim sum (drink tea) tomorrow?

7. Where do you want to go?

8. What do you like to eat?

LISTENING EXERCISE   *(CD 2, Track 27)*

I.   Listen to the dialogues and choose the correct answer

1. _____   2. _____   3. _____

4. _____   5. _____

II.   Listening comprehension

1. _____   2. _____

3. _____   4. _____

5. _____   6. _____

Lesson 11

Having A Chinese Dinner

CONVERSATION *(CD 2, Track 28)*

A. At a Chinese restaurant

Fùn-yìhng gwòng-làhm. Géi-dō wái a?
歡 迎 光 臨 。 幾 多 位 呀 ?
Welcome. How many persons?

Sei wái.
四 位 。
Four.

Chéng-mahn yáuh móuh dehng tói a?
請 問 有 冇 訂 枱 呀 ?
Have you made a reservation?

Yáuh.
有 。
Yes.

Gwai sing a?
貴 姓 呀 ?
May I know your name?

Sing Chàhn.
姓 陳 。
My name is Chan.

Chàhn sàang, m̀h-gòi nī-bihn lā.
陳 生 ， 唔 該 呢 邊 啦 。
Mr. Chan, this way please.

B.   Making order   *(CD 2, Track 29)*

Géi-wái yám dī māt-yéh a?
幾 位 飲 啲 乜 嘢 呀 ？
What would you like to drink?

Léuhng jì bē-jáu, yāt gwun hó-lohk, yāt bùi gwán-séui.
兩 枝 啤 酒 ， 一 罐 可 樂 ， 一 杯 滾 水 。
Two bottles of beer, a can of coke, a glass of boiled water.

M̀h-gòi bòng ngóh sé dī choi. Yiu yāt gàn baahk-cheuk-
hā, bun jek ja jí-gài, yāt go sài-làahn-fà cháau daai-jí
tùhng-màaih yùh-hèung ké-jí, haih gam dō la.
唔 該 幫 我 寫 啲 菜 。 要 一 斤 白 灼
蝦 ， 半 隻 炸 子 雞 ， 一 個 西 蘭 花 炒
帶 子 同 埋 魚 香 茄 子 ， 係 咁 多 喇 。
Please take my order. I would like to have a catty of steamed
shrimp, half a roast chicken, fried broccoli with scallop and
braised egg plant with spicy garlic paste. That's all.

Yiu m̀h-yiu tòng a?
要 唔 要 湯 呀 ？
Do you want any soup?

M̀h-sái la, m̀h-gòi.
唔 駛 喇 ， 唔 該 。
No. Thanks.

(Then the dishes come.)

Yiu géi-dō go faahn a?

要 幾 多 個 飯 呀 ?

How many bowls of rice do you want?

Sei go faahn lā, m̀h-gòi.

四 個 飯 啦 ， 唔 該 。

Four bowls of rice please.

(Saying to the others.)

Sihk-faahn. Yám-bùi.

食 飯 ， 飲 杯 。

Bon appetite. Cheers!

Yám-bùi.

飲 杯 。

Cheers!

C. During the dinner *(CD 2, Track 30)*

(Mr Chan tries to serve his guests.)

Jih-géi làih dāk la.

自 己 嚟 得 啦 。

We'll help ourselves.

Dī yéh láih chàih meih a?

啲 嘢 嚟 齊 未 呀 ?

Is everything you've ordered here?

Chàih la.

齊 喇 。

Yes, they're all here.

Yiu m̀h-yiu dī tìhm-bán a?

要 唔 要 啲 甜 品 呀？

Do you want some dessert?

M̀h-sái la. M̀h-gòi màaih-dāan.

唔 駛 喇 。 唔 該 埋 單 。

No. Check please.

M̀h-gòi béi jèung dāan ngóh.

Néih-deih sàu mh-sàu kāat ga?

唔 該 俾 張 單 我 。

你 哋 收 唔 收 卡 㗎 ？

Please give me the bill. Do you take credit card?

> kāat 卡 : the abbreviation of credit card 'seun-yuhng kāat' 信用卡.

Sàu.

收 。

Yes.

(CD 2, Track 31)

Cantonese Food Menu

Soup 湯 *(Tòng)*

Hói-sīn dauh-fuh gāng 海鮮豆腐羹	Seafood & beancurd soup
Gài-yùhng sūk-máih gāng 雞蓉粟米羹	Chicken & sweet corn soup
Laih-tòng 例湯	Soup of the day

Main dish 小菜 *(Síu choi)*

| Baahk-cheuk hà 白灼蝦 | Steamed shrimp |

Ja jí-gài 炸子雞	Roast chicken
Sài-làahn-fà cháau daai-jí 西蘭花炒帶子	Fried scallop w. broccoli
Syun-yùhng baahk-choi-jái 蒜蓉白菜仔	Fried pak-choi w. garlic
Yùh-hèung ké-jí 魚香茄子	Braised egg plant w. spicy garlic paste
Hàahm-yùh gài-nāp dauh-fuh bōu 鹹魚雞粒豆腐煲	Diced chicken & beancurd hot pot
Jìu-yìhm sìn-yáu 椒鹽鮮魷	Salt & pepper squid
Gwū-lōu-yuhk 咕嚕肉	Sweet & sour pork
Sūk-máih bāan faai 粟米斑塊	Garoupa fillet with sweet corn sauce

Dessert 甜品 *(Tìhm bán)*

Sàang-gwó ping-pún 生果拼盆 Fruit plate

VOCABULARY   *(CD 2, Track 32)*

1. bē-jáu 啤酒   N : beer
   (M: bùi 杯 / jì 枝 / gwun 罐)
   eg. yāt jì bē-jáu 一枝啤酒 : a bottle of beer
        yāt gwun bē-jáu 一罐啤酒 : a can of beer

2. dāan 單 (M: jèung 張)   N : bill; receipt; invoice

3. syù 書 (M: bún 本)   N : book
   *Yìng-màhn syù 英文書 : English book

4. bāt 筆 (M: jì 枝)   N : pen

5. jí 紙 (M: jèung 張)   N : paper

6. yàhn 人 (M: go 個)   N : people

7. bou-jí 報紙 (M: fahn 份)   N : newspaper

8. verb + jó 咗   VS : aspect of completion of
                                    action

9. kàhm-yaht 琴日   TW : yesterday

10. kàhm-máahn 琴晚   TW : last night

SENTENCE PATTERNS   (CD 2, Track 33)

A. Counting objects

☞   number + measure + noun
     數字 + 量詞 + 名詞

     eg. yāt go yàhn
          一   個   人
          (one person)

☞   géi (-dō) + measure + noun + a?
     幾（多） + 量詞 + 名詞 + 呀？

     eg. géi-dō go yàhn a?
          幾 多 個 人 呀 ？
          (How many people?)

1. Ngóh séung yiu yāt jì bāt.
    我 想 要 一 枝 筆 。

2. Kéuih sihk léuhng wún faahn.

佢 食 兩 碗 飯 。

3. Ngóh yáuh sàam go pàhng-yáuh làih yám chàh.

我 有 三 個 朋 友 嚟 飲 茶 。

4. Néih gūng-sī yáuh géi-dō go yàhn a?

你 公 司 有 幾 多 個 人 呀 ？

5. Ngóh séung máaih yāt bún syù.

我 想 買 一 本 書 。

6. Ngóh tái sei fahn bou-jí.

我 睇 四 份 報 紙 。

7. Mh-gòi ńgh bùi bē-jáu.

唔 該 五 杯 啤 酒 。

B. Action at recent past *(CD 2, Track 34)*

Affirmative statement :

☞ verb + jó (+ la) 動詞 ＋ 咗 （＋喇）

eg. Ngóh sihk-jó faahn la.

我 食 咗 飯 喇 。

(I have eaten already.)

Negative statement :

☞ móuh + verb 冇 ＋ 動詞

eg. Ngóh móuh sihk faahn.

我 冇 食 飯 。

(I didn't eat.)

Question form :

☞   Yáuh móuh + verb + a?   有冇 + 動詞 + 呀？

   eg.   Kéuih yáuh móuh sihk faahn a?
   佢　有　冇　食　飯　呀　？
   (Did he eat?)

   Answer: Yáuh. / Móuh.
   有　。 /　冇　。
   (Yes./No.)

1. Chàhn sàang yáuh móuh sihk-faahn a?
   陳　生　有　冇　食　飯　呀　？

2. Ngóh móuh yiu ga-fē, ngóh yiu nìhng-mūng-chàh.
   我　冇　要　咖　啡　，　我　要　檸　檬　茶　。

3. Néih kàhm-máahn yáuh móuh tái dihn-sih a?
   你　琴　晚　有　冇　睇　電　視　呀　？

4. Kéuih móuh dá dihn-wá béi Jèung síu-jé.
   佢　冇　打　電　話　畀　張　小　姐　。

5. Léih taai-táai yáuh móuh máaih-yéh a?
   李　太　太　有　冇　買　嘢　呀　？

6. Kéuih móuh làih yám chàh.
   佢　冇　嚟　飲　茶　。

7. Chàhn sìn-sàang yáuh móuh heui a?
   陳　先　生　有　冇　去　呀　？

8. Ngóh móuh tùhng kéuih sihk-faahn.
   我　冇　同　佢　食　飯　。

9. Ngóh máaih-jó yāt bún Yìng-màhn syù.

我 買 咗 一 本 英 文 書 。

10. Ngóh tái-jó nī-fahn bou-jí la.

我 睇 咗 呢 份 報 紙 喇 。

11. Kéuih tùhng bīn-go heui-jó máaih-yéh a?

佢 同 邊 個 去 咗 買 嘢 呀 ？

12. Ngóh-deih sihk-jó faahn la.

我 哋 食 咗 飯 喇 。

13. Ngóh pàhng-yáuh làih-jó ngóh ūk-kéi.

我 朋 友 嚟 咗 我 屋 企 。

14. Ngóh béi-jó yāt jì bāt, léuhng jèung jí kéuih.

我 畀 咗 一 枝 筆 ， 兩 張 紙 佢 。

15. Wòhng síu-jé jáu-jó la.

黃 小 姐 走 咗 喇 。

C. Need to : 'yiu' 要 **and 'm̀h-sái'** 唔駛   *(CD 2, Track 35)*

Affirmative statement :

☞ yiu + verb / noun 要 ＋ 動詞 / 名詞

eg. Ngóh yiu yám séui.

我 要 飲 水 。

(I need to drink water.)

Ngóh yiu séui.

我 要 水 。

(I want water.)

Negative statement :

☞ m̀h-yiu + noun 唔要 + 名詞

eg. Ngóh m̀h-yiu séui.
我 唔 要 水 。
(I don't want water.)

☞ m̀h-sái + verb 唔駛 + 動詞

eg. Ngóh m̀h-sái yám séui.
我 唔 駛 飲 水 。
(I don't need to drink water.)

Question form :

☞ yiu m̀h-yiu + noun + a? 要唔要 + 名詞 + 呀？

eg. Néih yiu m̀h yiu séui a?
你 要 唔 要 水 呀 ？
(Do you want any water?)

    Answer: Yiu. / M̀h-sái.
    要 。/ 唔駛 。
    (Yes./No.)

☞ sái m̀h-sái + verb + a? 駛唔駛 + 動詞 + 呀？

eg. Néih sái m̀h-sái yám séui a?
你 駛 唔 駛 飲 水 呀 ？
(Do you need to drink water?)

    Answer: Yiu. / M̀h-sái.
    要 。/ 唔駛 。
    (Yes./No.)

1. Ngóh yiu yāt bùi séui.
    我 要 一 杯 水 。

2. Néih tìng-yaht sái m̀h-sái fàan-gùng a?
    你 聽 日 駛 唔 駛 返 工 呀 ？

3. Chàhn síu-jé yiu m̀h-yiu syù a?
    陳 小 姐 要 唔 要 書 呀 ？

4. Ngóh m̀h-sái sihk-yéh, ngóh m̀h-tóuh-ngoh.
    我 唔 駛 食 嘢 ， 我 唔 肚 餓 。

5. Kéuih m̀h-yiu chàh, kéuih séung yiu dung séui.
    佢 唔 要 茶 ， 佢 想 要 凍 水 。

6. Ngóh chāt-dím-bun yiu fàan ūk-kéi.
    我 七 點 半 要 返 屋 企 。

7. Ngóh fong-gùng yiu tùhng taai-táai heui máaih-yéh.
    我 放 工 要 同 太 太 去 買 嘢 。

8. Kéuih-deih m̀h-sái daap-chè.
    佢 哋 唔 駛 搭 車 。

GUIDED CONVERSATION

Ordering food and drinks at a Chinese restaurant

Two students are at a Chinese restaurant and they are ordering some food. Another student acts as the waiter and asks what he/she would like to have and give suggestions.

Example:

1. Néih-deih yám m̀h-yám tòng a?
    你 哋 飲 唔 飲 湯 呀 ？
    Do you want to have some soup?

2. Séung yám māt-yéh tòng a?
想 飲 乜 嘢 湯 呀 ?
What kind of soup do you want?

3. Jùng m̀h-jùng-yi sihk baahk-cheuk-hà a?
鐘 唔 鐘 意 食 白 灼 蝦 呀 ?
Do you like to eat steamed shrimp?

4. Yáuh māt-yéh choi a?
有 乜 嘢 菜 呀 ?
What kind of vegetables do you have?

5. Dī yú leng-m̀h-leng a?
啲 魚 靚 唔 靚 呀 ?
Is the fish fresh?

PRACTICE

May I have a spoon?

eg. M̀h-gòi, ngóh séung yiu yāt jek gāng.
唔 該 , 我 想 要 一 隻 羹 。
Excuse me, I want a spoon.

Hóu a. Chéng dáng jahn.
好 呀 。 請 等 陣 。
OK. Please wait a moment.

Substitution

a) gāng 羹 (M: jek 隻) : spoon

b) faai-jí 筷子 (M: deui 對 / sèung 雙) : chopsticks

c) mòuh-gān 毛巾 (M: tìuh 條) : towel

d)   ngàh-chīm 牙籤 (M: jì 枝) : toothpicks

e)   wún 碗 (M: jek 隻 / go 個) : bowl

f)   hok 壳 (M: jek 隻 / go 個) : ladle

g)   bùi 杯 (M: jek 隻 / go 個) : cup; glass; mug

h)   yīn-fùi-gòng 煙灰缸 (M: go 個) : ashtray

i)   tói 枱 (M: jèung 張) : table

j)   dang 櫈 (M: jèung 張) : chair

PYRAMID DRILLS   *(CD 2, Track 36)*

1.   yāt jì bāt
                            一　枝　筆
                         yiu yāt jì bāt
                      要　一　枝　筆
                   séung yiu yāt jì bāt
                想　要　一　枝　筆
             Ngóh séung yiu yāt jì bāt.
          我　想　要　一　枝　筆　。

2.   heui
                            去
                         móuh heui
                      冇　去
                   yáuh móuh heui
                有　冇　去
             Léih sìn-sàang yáuh móuh heui a?
          李　先　生　有　冇　去　呀　?

3.   ngóh ūk-kéi
            我 屋 企

        làih ngóh ūk-kéi
        嚟 我 屋 企

      làih-jó ngóh ūk-kéi
      嚟 咗 我 屋 企

    pàhng-yáuh làih-jó ngóh ūk-kéi
    朋 友 嚟 咗 我 屋 企

  Ngóh pàhng-yáuh làih-jó ngóh ūk-kéi.
  我 朋 友 嚟 咗 我 屋 企。

4.   fàan-gùng
            返 工

        tìng-yaht fàan-gùng
        聽 日 返 工

      tìng-yaht m̀h-sái fàan-gùng
      聽 日 唔 駛 返 工

    Néih tìng-yaht m̀h-sái fàan-gùng
    你 聽 日 唔 駛 返 工

  Néih tìng-yaht sái m̀h-sái fàan-gùng a?
  你 聽 日 駛 唔 駛 返 工 呀?

SUBSTITUTION DRILLS   *(CD 2, Track 37)*

1. Néih gàm-yaht yáuh móuh fàan-gùng a?
    你 今 日 有 冇 返工 呀?

    a) daap síu-bā 搭小巴   *b)* tái bou-jí 睇報紙

    c) heui 去   *d)* yám chàh 飲茶

2. Kéuih béi-jó yāt-bún syù ngóh.
   佢 畀 咗 一 本 書 我 。

   a) sàam jì bāt 三枝筆   b) léuhng jèung jí 兩張紙

   c) sei fahn bou-jí 四份報紙   d) $200

3. Wòhng síu-jé yiu yám bē-jáu.
   黃 小 姐 要 飲 啤 酒 。

   a) tái bou-jí 睇報紙   b) fan-gaau 瞓覺

   c) ńgh-dím jáu 五點走   d) sihk faahn 食飯

4. Chàhn sìn-sàang m̀h-sái sihk yéh.
   陳 先 生 唔 駛 食 嘢 。

   a) fàan ūk-kéi 返屋企   b) daap bā-sí 搭巴士

   c) máaih syù 買書   d) máaih bou-jí 買報紙

REVIEW EXERCISE

Translation

1. Please give me this book.

2. I didn't go there.

3. My friend slept at 11:15 last night.

4. Please give him today's newspaper.

5. His wife doesn't need to buy anything.

6. I drank two cups of tea.

7. Who do you give the pen to?

8. I gave you 10 sheets of paper.

9. Tomorrow I have to go home for dinner.

10. We didn't take any transport.

LISTENING EXERCISE   *(CD 2, Track 38)*

Listen to the dialogues and choose the correct answer

1. _____   2. _____   3. _____   4. _____

5. _____   6. _____   7. _____   8. _____

Lesson 12

Where Do You Live?

A. Where do you work?

Néih hái bīn-douh fàan-gùng a?

你 喺 邊 度 返 工 呀 ?

Where do you work?

Ngóh hái Wāan-jái fàan-gùng.

我 喺 灣 仔 返 工 。

I work in Wan Chai.

Wāan-jái bīn-douh a?

灣 仔 邊 度 呀 ?

Where in Wan Chai?

Hái Jùng-wàahn Gwóng-chèuhng.

喺 中 環 廣 場 。

At Central Plaza.

Géi-dō láu a?

幾 多 樓 呀 ?

Which floor?

Sahp baat láu.
十 八 樓 。
On the 18th floor.

B.   Where do you live?   *(CD 2, Track 40)*

Hi! Hóu noih móuh gin. Néih yìh-gā hái bīn-douh jyuh a?
嗨 ！ 好 耐 冇 見 。 你 而 家 喺 邊 度 住 呀 ？
Hey! Haven't seen you for a long time. Where do you live now?

Ngóh hái Tùhng-lòh-wāan jyuh.
我 喺 銅 鑼 灣 住 。
I live in Causeway Bay.

Tùhng-lòh-wāan hóu fòng-bihn wo.
銅 鑼 灣 好 方 便 喎 。
Causeway Bay is a convenient place.

Haih a. Jàn-haih hóu fòng-bihn.
係 呀 。 眞 係 好 方 便 。
Yes. It's really convenient.

Gám, néih hái bīn-douh fàan-gùng a?
咁 ， 你 喺 邊 度 返 工 呀 ？
Well, where do you work?

Ngóh hái Jùng-wàahn.
我 喺 中 環 。
I work in Central.

Ngóh dōu haih wo. Dāk-hàahn yāt-chàih sihk faahn lā.

我 都 係 喎 。 得 閒 一 齊 食 飯 啦 。

Me too. Let's have lunch together when you are free.

C. Where shall we go for lunch? *(CD 2, Track 41)*

Ngóh-deih heui bīn-douh sihk aan a?

我 哋 去 邊 度 食 晏 呀 ?

Where shall we go for lunch?

Heui Méih-sām Jáu-làuh hóu m̀h-hóu a?

去 美 心 酒 樓 , 好 唔 好 呀 ?

Shall we go to Maxim's Restaurant?

Hóu a. Hái géi-dō láu ga?

好 呀 。 喺 幾 多 樓 㗎 ?

Fine. On which floor?

Sàam láu.

三 樓 。

On the 3rd floor.

Géi-dō dím a?

幾 多 點 呀 ?

What time?

Yāt-dím lā.

一 點 啦 。

At 1:00.

READING *(CD 2, Track 42)*

Ngóh haih Chàhn Ji-Mìhng, jyuh hái Wāan-jái, gūng-sī hái
我 係 陳 志 明 ， 住 喺 灣 仔 ， 公 司 喺
I am Chan Chi Ming. I live in Wan Chai. My office is in

Tùhng-lòh-wāan. Ngóh múih-yāht daap síu-bā fàan-gùng. Ngóh
銅 鑼 灣 。 我 每 日 搭 小 巴 返 工 。 我
Causeway Bay. Everyday I go to work by mini-bus. I have

yāt-dím sihk-faahn, jeui jùng-yi tùhng tùhng-sih heui yám chàh.
一 點 食 飯 ， 最 鍾 意 同 同 事 去 飲 茶 。
lunch at 1:00. I like to go for tea with my colleagues the best.

Ngóh-deih sìh-sìh hái Méih-Sām Jáu-làuh yám-chàh.
我 哋 時 時 喺 美 心 酒 樓 飲 茶 。
We often go to Maxim's Restaurant to have tea.

Méih-Sām ge dím-sām hóu hóu-sihk. Ngóh luhk-dím fong-gùng.
美 心 嘅 點 心 好 好 食 。 我 六 點 放 工 。
The dim sum at Maxim's are very delicious. I finish work at 6:00.

Yeh-máahn ngóh hái ūk-kéi sihk-faahn.
夜 晚 我 喺 屋 企 食 飯 。
In the evening, I eat at home.

VOCABULARY *(CD 2, Track 43)*

1. Jùng-wàahn 中環   PW : Central
2. Gām-jūng 金鐘   PW : Admiralty
3. Wāan-jái 灣仔   PW : Wan Chai

4. Tùhng-lòh-wāan or   PW : Causeway Bay
   Tùhng-lòh-wàahn 銅鑼灣

5. Jìm-sà-jéui 尖沙咀   PW : Tsim Sha Tsui

6. jyuh 住   V : live

7. sé-jih-làuh 寫字樓 (M: go 個) PW : office

8. jáu-làuh 酒樓 (M: gàan 間)   PW : Chinese restaurant

9. hái 喺   P : located at, in or on

10. láu 樓   N : floor

    eg. gáu láu 九樓 : 9th floor
        deih-há 地下 : ground floor

11. mùhn-háu 門口 (M: go 個)   N : entrance; doorway

12. jàn-haih 眞係   ADV : really

13. fòng-bihn 方便   ADJ : convenient

14. wo 喎   FP : implies telling new
                                      situation; to remind

SENTENCE PATTERNS   (CD 2, Track 44)

A. Subject + place + verb

Affirmative statement :

☞ Subject + hái + place + verb
   主詞 + 喺 + 地方 + 動詞

   eg. Ngóh hái Wāan-jái fàan-gùng.
        我 喺 灣 仔 返 工 。
        (I work in Wan Chai.)

Negative statement :

☞   Subject + m̀h-hái + place + verb

主詞 ＋ 唔喺 ＋ 地方 ＋ 動詞

eg.   Ngóh m̀h-hái Wāan-jái fàan-gùng.

我 唔 喺 灣 仔 返 工 。

(I don't work in Wan Chai.)

Question form :

☞   Subject + hái bīn-douh + verb + a?

主詞 ＋ 喺邊度 ＋ 動詞 ＋ 呀 ？

eg.   Néih hái bīn-douh fàan-gùng a?

你 喺 邊 度 返 工 呀 ？

(Where do you work?)

1.   Ngóh-deih ge gūng-sī hái Wāan-jái.

我 哋 嘅 公 司 喺 灣 仔 。

2.   Hòh síu-jé hái Tùhng-lòh-wāan máaih-yéh.

何 小 姐 喺 銅 鑼 灣 買 嘢 。

3.   Kéuih-ge sé-jih-làuh hái Gām-jūng Taai-gwú Gwóng-chèuhng. (*Pacific Place)

佢 嘅 寫 字 樓 喺 金 鐘 太 古 廣 場 。

4.   Dihn-wá hái gó-douh.

電 話 喺 嗰 度 。

5.   Kéuih jùng-yi hái Jìm-sà-jéui yám-chàh.

佢 鍾 意 喺 尖 沙 咀 飲 茶 。

6.   Néih-deih hái bīn-douh sihk-faahn a?

你 哋 喺 邊 度 食 飯 呀 ？

7. Ngóh ge sé-jih-làuh hái yah-yih láu.

   我　嘅　寫　字　樓　喺　廿　二　樓　。

8. Kéuih hái bīn-douh jyuh a?

   佢　喺　邊　度　住　呀　？

9. Ngóh hái mùhn-háu dáng néih.

   我　喺　門　口　等　你　。

10. Néih hái bīn-douh daap-chè fàan ūk-kéi a?

   你　喺　邊　度　搭　車　返　屋　企　呀　？

B.　Subject + time + place + verb　*(CD 2, Track 45)*

☞　Subject + time + place + verb

　　主詞 + 時間 + 地方 + 動詞

eg.　Ngóh yāt-dím hái Jùng-wàahn sihk aan.

　　我　一　點　喺　中　環　食　晏　。

　　(I have lunch in Central at 1:00.)

1. Ngóh yìh-gā hái ūk-kéi tái dihn-sih.

   我　而　家　喺　屋　企　睇　電　視　。

2. Néih-deih gàm-yaht hái bīn-douh sihk-faahn a?

   你　哋　今　日　喺　邊　度　食　飯　呀　？

3. Ngóh hái jáu-làuh dá dihn-wá béi néih.

   我　喺　酒　樓　打　電　話　畀　你　。

4. Néih yìh-gā hái bīn-douh a?

   你　而　家　喺　邊　度　呀　？

5. Ngóh-deih ńgh-dím-sei hái Sùhng-gwòng (*Sogo Department Store) mùhn-háu dáng.

我 哋 五 點 四 喺 崇 光 門 口 等 。

6. Gàm-yaht hái bīn-douh yám-chàh a?

今 日 喺 邊 度 飲 茶 呀 ？

7. Néih géi dím hái ūk-kéi a?

你 幾 點 喺 屋 企 呀 ？

8. Kéuih léuhng-dím-bun hái Gām-jūng.

佢 兩 點 半 喺 金 鐘 。

C. Giving suggestion (CD 2, Track 46)

☞ Suggestion + hóu m̀h-hóu a?

建議 + 好唔好呀 ？ (Is it fine?/Is that alright?)

eg. Sàam-dím, hóu m̀h-hóu a?

三 點 ， 好 唔 好 呀 ？

(How about 3:00?)

Answer: Hóu. / M̀h-hóu.

好 。/ 唔 好 。

(Fine./No.)

1. Ngóh-deih heui yám chàh, hóu m̀h-hóu a?

我 哋 去 飲 茶 ， 好 唔 好 呀 ？

2. Móuh ga-fē, yám séui hóu m̀h-hóu a?

冇 咖 啡 ， 飲 水 好 唔 好 呀 ？

3. Gàm-yaht yāt-chàih sihk-faahn, hóu m̀h-hóu a?

今 日 一 齊 食 飯 ， 好 唔 好 呀 ？

4. Ngóh-deih hái mùhn-háu dáng, hóu m̀h-hóu a?
    我 哋 喺 門 口 等 ， 好 唔 好 呀 ？

5. Yám hó-lohk, hóu m̀h-hóu a?
    飲 可 樂 ， 好 唔 好 呀 ？

6. Ngóh-deih yāt-chàih heui máaih-yéh, hóu m̀h-hóu a?
    我 哋 一 齊 去 買 嘢 ， 好 唔 好 呀 ？

7. Heui gó-douh yám chàh, hóu m̀h-hóu a?
    去 嗰 度 飲 茶 ， 好 唔 好 呀 ？

8. Máaih nī-go hóu m̀h-hóu a?
    買 呢 個 好 唔 好 呀 ？

PYRAMID DRILLS   *(CD 2, Track 47)*

1.   Tùhng-lòh-wāan
                              銅 鑼 灣
                        hái Tùhng-lòh-wāan
                          喺 銅 鑼 灣
                      hái Tùhng-lòh-wāan jyuh
                        喺 銅 鑼 灣 住
                    Kéuih hái Tùhng-lòh-wāan jyuh
                      佢 喺 銅 鑼 灣 住
                  Kéuih m̀h-hái Tùhng-lòh-wāan jyuh.
                    佢 唔 喺 銅 鑼 灣 住 。

2.   Wāan-jái
                              灣 仔
                          hái Wāan-jái
                          喺 灣 仔

hái Wāan-jái máaih-yéh

喺 灣 仔 買 嘢

kàhm-yaht hái Wāan-jái máaih-yéh

琴 日 喺 灣 仔 買 嘢

Néih kàhm-yaht hái Wāan-jái máaih-yéh

你 琴 日 喺 灣 仔 買 嘢

Néih kàhm-yaht tùhng pàhng-yáuh hái Wāan-jái máaih-yéh.

你 琴 日 同 朋 友 喺 灣 仔 買 嘢 。

SUBSTITUTION DRILLS   *(CD 2, Track 48)*

1. Ngóh hái <u>Jùng-wàahn</u> jyuh. 我喺中環住 。

    a) Jìm-sà-jéui 尖沙咀   *b)* luhk láu 六樓

    c) deih-há 地下   *d)* Tùhng-lòh-wāan 銅鑼灣

2. Kéuih kàhm-yaht hái Gām-jūng <u>máaih-yéh</u>.

    佢琴日喺金鐘買嘢 。

    a) yám-chàh 飲茶   *b)* sihk aan 食晏

    c) fàan-gùng 返工   *d)* dá dihn-wá béi ngóh 打電話畀我

REVIEW EXERCISE

I.   Rewrite the following sentences

1. ngóh / sahp baat / hái / láu / sé-jih-làuh / ge

    我 / 十 八 / 喺 / 樓 / 寫 字 樓 / 嘅

2. bīn-douh / a / néih / hái / jyuh

    邊 度 / 呀 / 你 / 喺 / 住

3. gūng-sī / Jùng-wàahn / nī-gàan / hái / m̀h
公 司 / 中 環 / 呢 間 / 喺 / 唔

4. bīn-go / a / fáan-gùng / hái / Wāan-jái
邊 個 / 呀 / 返 工 / 喺 / 灣 仔

5. ge / Jìm-sà-jéui / pàhng-yáuh / jyuh / ngóh / hái
嘅 / 尖 沙 咀 / 朋 友 / 住 / 我 / 喺

6. chàh / Léih sìn-sàang / láu / sàam / hái / yám
茶 / 李 先 生 / 樓 / 三 / 喺 / 飲

7. jyuh / ngóh / hái / Tùhng-lòh-wāan / m̀h
住 / 我 / 喺 / 銅 鑼 灣 / 唔

II. Translation

1. Do you like this Chinese restaurant?

2. I live in Tsim Sha Tsui.

3. Where does your friend work?

4. I eat at home today.

5. Where were you at 2:30?

6. My office is on the 25th floor.

7. I have dinner with my friends in Wan Chai.

8. Where was Mr. Chan yesterday?

9. I go shopping in Causeway Bay.

10. Where is your office?

11. What time shall we meet at the entrance?

12. My wife's office is not in Admiralty.

III. Study the plan of this department store, answer the questions *(CD 2, Track 49)*

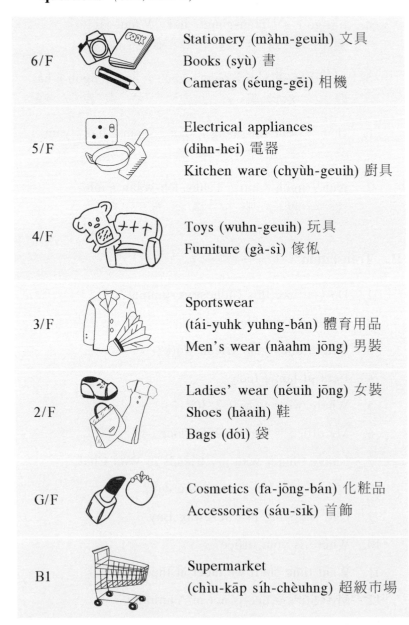

6/F	Stationery (màhn-geuih) 文具 Books (syù) 書 Cameras (séung-gēi) 相機
5/F	Electrical appliances (dihn-hei) 電器 Kitchen ware (chyùh-geuih) 廚具
4/F	Toys (wuhn-geuih) 玩具 Furniture (gà-sì) 傢俬
3/F	Sportswear (tái-yuhk yuhng-bán) 體育用品 Men's wear (nàahm jōng) 男裝
2/F	Ladies' wear (néuih jōng) 女裝 Shoes (hàaih) 鞋 Bags (dói) 袋
G/F	Cosmetics (fa-jōng-bán) 化粧品 Accessories (sáu-sīk) 首飾
B1	Supermarket (chìu-kāp síh-chèuhng) 超級市場

1. Sàam láu haih m̀h-haih chìu-kāp síh-chèuhng a?

    三 樓 係 唔 係 超 級 市 場 呀 ？

2. Ngóh taai-táai yiu máaih hàaih, heui géi-dō láu a?

    我 太 太 要 買 鞋 ， 去 幾 多 樓 呀 ？

3. Fa-jōng-bán haih m̀h-haih hái deih-há a?

    化 粧 品 係 唔 係 喺 地 下 呀 ？

4. Ngóh séung máaih wuhn-geuih, heui sei láu ngāam m̀h-
    ngāam (*correct) a?

    我 想 買 玩 具 ， 去 四 樓 啱 唔 啱 呀 ？

5. Ngóh hóu tóuh-ngoh, ngóh séung máaih yéh sihk, ngóh
    heui géi-dō láu a?

    我 好 肚 餓 ， 我 想 買 嘢 食 ， 我 去 幾 多
    樓 呀 ？

6. Tùhng jōng (*Children's wear) hái géi-dō láu a?

    童 裝 喺 幾 多 樓 呀 ？

7. Ńgh láu yáuh móuh wún maaih (*sell) a?

    五 樓 有 冇 碗 賣 呀 ？

8. Ngóh séung máaih yāt go dói, heui yih láu ngāam m̀h-
    ngāam a?

    我 想 買 一 個 袋 ， 去 二 樓 啱 唔 啱
    呀 ？

9. Máaih bāt máaih syù, heui géi-dō láu a?

    買 筆 買 書 ， 去 幾 多 樓 呀 ？

10. Hái géi-dō láu yáuh dihn-sih maaih a?

    喺 幾 多 樓 有 電 視 賣 呀 ？

IV.　Make conversations to invite your friends

Example:

Ngóh-deih heui <u>yám chàh</u>, hóu m̀h-hóu a?
我　地　去　飲　茶　，　好　唔　好　呀　？

Hóu a. Géi-dō dím heui a?
好　呀　。　幾　多　點　去　呀　？

<u>Sahp-yih-dím-bun</u> hóu m̀h-hóu a?
十　二　點　半　好　唔　好　呀　？

Hóu. Ngóh-deih hái <u>Sùhng-gwòng</u> (*Sogo Department Store) dáng lā.
好　。　我　哋　喺　崇　光　等　啦　。

Hóu lā. Yāt-jahn gin. (*See you later)
好　啦　。　一　陣　見　。

Substitution

a)　máaih-yéh 買嘢
　　2:45
　　Tīn-sīng Máh-Tàuh 天星碼頭：Star Ferry

b)　yám yéh 飲嘢
　　5:30
　　Ji-deih Gwóng-chèuhng pan-séui chìh
　　置地廣場噴水池：the fountain in Landmark

c)　sihk-fahhn 食飯
　　1:00
　　Deih-tit-jaahm Hàhng-sāng Ngàhn-hòhng
　　地鐵站恒生銀行：Hang Seng Bank at MTR station

d)   yám chàh 飲茶
    9:30
    Méih-sām Jáu-làuh 美心酒樓：Maxim's Restaurant

LISTENING EXERCISE   *(CD 2, Track 50)*

I.   Listen to the dialogues and answer the questions

1. _____   2. _____

3. _____   4. _____

5. _____   6. _____

7. _____   8. _____

II.   Choose the appropriate Cantonese translation

1.   He doesn't live in Causeway Bay.   _____

2.   My office is on the 24/F.   _____

3.   I like this Chinese restaurant.   _____

Lesson 13

Weather and Date

CONVERSATION   *(CD 2, Track 51)*

A. It may rain tomorrow

 Tìng-yaht fong-ga, ngóh-deih heui léuih-hàhng, hóu m̀h-hóu a?

聽 日 放 假 ， 我 哋 去 旅 行 ， 好 唔 好 呀 ？

Tomorrow is a holiday, shall we go on an outing?

 Daahn-haih tìng-yaht tìn-hei màh-má-déi, waahk-jé lohk-yúh.

但 係 聽 日 天 氣 麻 麻 哋 ， 或 者 落 雨 。

However, the weather tomorrow is not very good maybe it will rain.

 Gám, ngóh-deih hah-go láih-baai heui, hóu m̀h-hóu a?

咁 ， 我 哋 下 個 禮 拜 去 ， 好 唔 好 呀 ？

Well, shall we go next week?

Hóu a. Hah-go láih-baai ge tìn-hei wúih hóu-gwo gàm-
go láih-baai gwa.

好 呀 。 下 個 禮 拜 嘅 天 氣 會 好 過
今 個 禮 拜 啩 。

OK. I guess the weather next week will be better than this
week.

B. There will be a meeting on the 18th of June *(CD 2, Track 52)*

Luhk-yuht sahp-baat-houh hòi-wúi.

六 月 十 八 號 開 會 。

There will be a meeting on 18th June.

Sahp-baat-houh haih sìng-kèih-géi a?

十 八 號 係 星 期 幾 呀 ？

What day is the 18th.

Sìng-kèih-yih.

星 期 二 。

It's a Tuesday.

Géi dím hòi-wúi a?

幾 點 開 會 呀 ？

What time is the meeting?

Sàam-dím. Gei-dāk làih a!

三 點 。 記 得 嚟 呀 ！

At 3:00. Remember to come.

Dāk la. Ngóh gei-dāk làih la.

得 喇 。 我 記 得 嚟 喇 。

OK. I'll remember to come.

READING   *(CD 2, Track 53)*

Ngóh m̀h-jùng-yi Hèung-góng ge tìn-hei, hóu síu hóu-tìn.
我　唔　鍾　意　香　港　嘅　天　氣　，　好　少　好　天　。
I dislike the weather in Hong Kong. There's seldom any good weather.

Hèung-góng ge tìn-hei, sàam-sei-yuht hóu sāp, sìh-sìh
香　港　嘅　天　氣　，　三　、　四　月　好　濕　，　時　時
The weather in March and April in Hong Kong is humid. It's often

yàm-tìn tùhng lohk-yúh, jàn-haih hóu màh-fàahn. Ńgh-yuht ji
陰　天　同　落　雨　，　眞　係　好　麻　煩　。　五　月　至
cloudy or rainy. There's so much trouble. May through

gáu-yuht hóu yiht, sìh-sìh lohk yúh. Sahp-yāt-yuht ge tìn-hei
九　月　好　熱　，　時　時　落　雨　。　十　一　月　嘅　天　氣
September it's hot and often rains. The weather in November is

jeui hóu, daahn-haih sahp-yih-yuht, yāt-yuht yáuh-sìh hóu dung.
最　好　，　但　係　十　二　月　、　一　月　有　時　好　凍　。
best, but sometimes it is very cold in December and January.

Ngóh m̀h-jùng-yi dung.
我　唔　鍾　意　凍　。
I dislike cold weather.

VOCABULARY   *(CD 2, Track 54)*

1. tìn-hei 天氣　　　　N : weather

2. hóu-tìn 好天　　　　ADJ : fine weather

3. lohk yúh 落雨　　　VO : rain

4. yàm-tìn 陰天　　　　N : cloudy

5. yuht 月   TW : month
   * yāt-yuht 一月 ：January
   * yih-yuht 二月 ：February
   * sahp-yuht 十月 ：October
   * sahp-yih-yuht 十二月 ：December
   * géi(-dō)-yuht 幾多月 / bīn-go yuht 邊個月 ：which month
   * seuhng-go yuht 上個月 ：last month
   * nī-go yuht 呢個月 / gàm-go yuht 今個月 ：this month
   * hah-go yuht 下個月 ：next month

6. houh 號   TW : date of a month

7. géi-sìh 幾時   TW : when

8. léuih-hàhng 旅行   N : travel; trip; picnic; outing

9. fong-ga 放假   VO : on holiday; on vacation; on leave

10. wáan 玩   V : to enjoy; to play

11. hòi-wúi 開會   VO : to hold or attend a meeting

12. gei-dāk 記得   V : remember
    * m̀h-gei-dāk 唔記得 ：forget

13. jì 知   V : to know a fact

14. faai 快   ADJ : fast; quick

15. syù-fuhk 舒服   ADJ : comfortable
    * m̀h-syù-fuhk 唔舒服 ：uncomfortable; sick

16. màh-fàahn 麻煩   ADJ : troublesome

17. daahn-haih 但係   CON : but; however

18. ADJ + gwo 過   P : more than

19. jeui 最   P : most

20. ji 至   CON : until; to

21. sìh-sìh 時時   A : very often, always

22. yáuh-sìh 有時   A : some times

23. hóu-síu 好少   A : seldom; rarely

24. Hèung-góng 香港   PW : Hong Kong

SENTENCE PATTERNS   *(CD 2, Track 55)*

A. Days of the Week

Sìng-kéih-yaht / Láih-baai-yaht	: Sunday
星 期 日 / 禮 拜 日	
Sìng-kéih-yāt / Láih-baai-yāt	: Monday
星 期 一 / 禮 拜 一	
Sìng-kéih-yih / Láih-baai-yih	: Tuesday
星 期 二 / 禮 拜 二	
Sìng-kéih-sàam / Láih-baai-sàam	: Wednesday
星 期 三 / 禮 拜 三	
Sìng-kéih-sei / Láih-baai-sei	: Thursday
星 期 四 / 禮 拜 四	
Sìng-kéih-ńgh / Láih-baai-ńgh	: Friday
星 期 五 / 禮 拜 五	
Sìng-kéih-luhk / Láih-baai-luhk	: Saturday
星 期 六 / 禮 拜 六	
Seuhng-go sìng-kèih / Seuhng-go láih-baai	: last week
上 個 星 期 / 上 個 禮 拜	
Nī-go sìng-kèih / Gàm-go láih-baai	: this week
呢 個 星 期 / 今 個 禮 拜	
Hah-go sìng-kèih / Hah-go láih-baai	: next week
下 個 星 期 / 下 個 禮 拜	
Seuhng-go sìng-kèih-luhk	: last Saturday
上 個 星 期 六	

PRACTICE *(CD 2, Track 56)*

Use the following table and answer the questions

	Mon	Tue	Wed	Thu	Fri	Sat	Sun
Last week	31 ℃	28 ℃	30 ℃	28 ℃	29 ℃	32 ℃	27 ℃
This week	20 ℃	18 ℃	19 ℃	17 ℃	16 ℃	18 ℃	25 ℃
Next Week	26 ℃	22 ℃	23 ℃	29 ℃	30 ℃	33 ℃	21 ℃

* Gàm-yaht haih sìng-kèih-sàam. Gàm-yaht sahp-gáu douh
  (*degree).
  今 日 係 星 期 三 。 今 日 十 九 度 。

1. Kàhm-yaht géi-dō douh a?
   琴 日 幾 多 度 呀 ？

2. Sìng-kèih-yāt géi-dō douh a?
   星 期 一 幾 多 度 呀 ？

3. Seuhng-go láih-baai-luhk géi-dō douh a?
   上 個 禮 拜 六 幾 多 度 呀 ？

4. Hah-go láih-baai-yih géi-dō douh a?
   下 個 禮 拜 二 幾 多 度 呀 ？

5. Láih-baai-yaht géi-dō douh a?
   禮 拜 日 幾 多 度 呀 ？

6. Sìng-kèih-ńgh haih m̀h-haih yih-sahp-gáu douh a?
   星 期 五 係 唔 係 二 十 九 度 呀 ？

7. Seuhng-go sìng-kèih hóu yiht, haih m̀h-haih a?
   上 個 星 期 好 熱 ， 係 唔 係 呀 ？

8. Sìng-kèih-yih haih m̀h-haih yih sahp douh a?

星　期　二　係　唔　係　二　十　度　呀　？

9. Tìng-yaht géi-dō douh a?

聽　日　幾　多　度　呀　？

10. Hah-go láih-baai dung m̀h-dung a?

下　個　禮　拜　凍　唔　凍　呀　？

B. Date　*(CD 2, Track 57)*

1. Sìng-kèih-luhk-yaht fong-ga.

星　期　六　、　日　放　假　。

2. Kéuih seuhng-go-yuht heui-jó léuih-hàhng.

佢　上　個　月　去　咗　旅　行　。

3. Ngóh-deih ńgh-yuht sahp-chāt-houh sàam-dím hòi-wúi.

我　哋　五　月　十　七　號　三　點　開　會　。

4. Baat-yuht yah-sàam-houh fong-ga. Jì m̀h-jì fong māt-yéh ga a?

八　月　廿　三　號　放　假　。　知　唔　知　放　乜　嘢　假　呀　？

5. Sahp-yāt-yuht ńgh-houh heui sihk-faahn.

十　一　月　五　號　去　食　飯　。

6. Hah-go sìng-kèih-luhk haih sei-yuht sahp-luhk-houh.

下　個　星　期　六　係　四　月　十　六　號　。

7. Sahp-yuht yāt-houh fong ga.

十　月　一　號　放　假　。

8. Chāt-yuht yah-yih-houh heui léuih-hàhng.

七　月　廿　二　號　去　旅　行　。

9. Néih géi-sìh làih nī-gàan gūng-sī ga?

    你 幾 時 嚟 呢 間 公 司 㗎 ？

10. Kéuih pàhng-yáuh géi-sìh heui léuih-hàhng a?

    佢 朋 友 幾 時 去 旅 行 呀 ？

11. Néih géi-sìh heui kéuih ūk-kéi wáan ga?

    你 幾 時 去 佢 屋 企 玩 㗎 ？

12. Néih géi-sìh heui Jìm-sà-jéui máaih-yéh a?

    你 幾 時 去 尖 沙 咀 買 嘢 呀 ？

13. Néih géi-sìh máaih syù a?

    你 幾 時 買 書 呀 ？

14. Néih géi-sìh dāk-hàahn yāt-chàih (*together) sihk-faahn a?

    你 幾 時 得 閒 一 齊 食 飯 呀 ？

15. Néih ge dihn-sih géi-sìh máaih ga?

    你 嘅 電 視 幾 時 買 㗎 ？

PRACTICE

I. Ask each other's birthday

Néih géi-sìh sàang-yaht a?

你 幾 時 生 日 呀 ？

(When is your birthday?)

Ngóh yāt-yuht yāt-houh sàang-yaht.

我 一 月 一 號 生 日 。

(My birthday January 1st.)

II. Use the given information and answer the questions

(CD 2, Track 58)

Sun	Mon	Tue	Wed	Thu	Fri	Sat
				1 ☀	2 ☀	3 ☁
4 ☁	5 ☁	6 ☔	7 ☀	8 ☀	9 ☀	10 ☀
11 ☁	12 ☔	13 ☔	14 ☔	15 ☔	16 ☁	17 ☁
18 ☀	19 ☀	20 ☀	21 ☀	22 ☁	23 ☔	24 ☁
25 ☁	26 ☁	27 ☀	28 ☀	29 ☀	30 ☔	

* Gàm-yaht haih yah-yih houh, yàm-tìn.

今 日 係 廿 二 號 ， 陰 天 。

1. Sìng-kèih-yāt hóu m̀h-hóu-tìn a?

   星 期 一 好 唔 好 天 呀 ？

2. Sìng-kèih-yih yáuh móuh lohk-yúh a?

   星 期 二 有 冇 落 雨 呀 ？

3. Sahp-sàam-houh haih m̀h-haih yàm-tìn a?

   十 三 號 係 唔 係 陰 天 呀 ？

4. Chāt-houh ji sahp-houh haih m̀h-haih hóu-tìn a?

   七 號 至 十 號 係 唔 係 好 天 呀 ？

5. Seuhng-go láih-baai-sàam haih m̀h-haih yàm-tìn a?

   上 個 禮 拜 三 係 唔 係 陰 天 呀 ？

6. Yih-sahp-gáu-houh lohk-yúh àh?

   二 十 九 號 落 雨 吖 ？

7. Yih-sahp-houh tùhng yih-sahp-sei-houh hóu-tìn àh?

二 十 號 同 二 十 四 號 好 天 吓？

8. Yāt-houh yáuh móuh lohk-yùh a?

一 號 有 冇 落 雨 呀？

9. Kàhm-yaht hóu m̀h-hóu-tìn a?

琴 日 好 唔 好 天 呀？

10. Tìng-yaht haih m̀h-haih yàm-tìn a?

聽 日 係 唔 係 陰 天 呀？

C. How often *(CD 2, Track 59)*

☞ Subject + adverb of frequency + time + place + verb

主語 + 副詞 + 時間詞 + 地方 + 動詞

1. Ngóh sìh-sìh tùhng tùhng-sih heui yám-chàh.

我 時 時 同 同 事 去 飲 茶。

2. Ngóh ūk-kéi yáuh-sìh chāt-dím-bun sihk-faahn, yáuh-sìh baat-dím sihk-faahn.

我 屋 企 有 時 七 點 半 食 飯，有 時 八 點 食 飯。

3. Kéuih hóu-síu heui léuih-hàhng.

佢 好 少 去 旅 行。

4. Néih haih m̀h-haih sìh-sìh sahp-yāt-dím fan-gaau ga?

你 係 唔 係 時 時 十 一 點 瞓 覺 㗎？

5. Ngóh-deih yáuh-sìh hái gūng-sī sihk aan.

我 哋 有 時 喺 公 司 食 晏。

6. Ngóh hóu-síu tái dihn-sih, ngóh m̀h-jùng-yi tái.

我 好 少 睇 電 視，我 唔 鍾 意 睇。

7. Kéuih yáuh-sìh daap síu-bā, yáuh-sìh daap dīk-sí fàan-gùng.

佢 有 時 搭 小 巴 ， 有 時 搭 的 士 返 工 。

8. Ngóh-deih hóu-síu daap bā-sī fàan ūk-kéi, yàn-waih (*because) hóu màh-fàahn.

我 哋 好 少 搭 巴 士 返 屋 企 ， 因 爲 好 麻 煩 。

9. Ngóh sìh-sìh baat-gáu-dím hái gūng-sī jáu.

我 時 時 八 、 九 點 喺 公 司 走 。

10. Kéuih hóu-síu hái sé-jih-làuh. Ngóh sìh-sìh dá dihn-wá béi kéuih, kéuih dōu (*always) m̀h-hái-douh.

佢 好 少 喺 寫 字 樓 。 我 時 時 打 電 話 畀 佢 ， 佢 都 唔 喺 度 。

D. Until, to : 'ji' 至 *(CD 2, Track 60)*

1. Sahp-houh ji sahp-luhk-houh fong-ga.

十 號 至 十 六 號 放 假 。

2. Sìng-kéih-yāt ji sìng-kéih-sàam, ngóh m̀h-dāk-hàahn.

星 期 一 至 星 期 三 ， 我 唔 得 閒 。

3. Sahp-yih-dím ji yāt-dím-bun sihk-faahn.

十 二 點 至 一 點 半 食 飯 。

4. Ngóh kàhm-máahn baat-dím ji sahp-dím hái ūk-kéi tái dihn-sih.

我 琴 晚 八 點 至 十 點 喺 屋 企 睇 電 視 。

5. Ngóh ńgh-houh ji baat-houh heui léuih-hàhng.

我 五 號 至 八 號 去 旅 行 。

6. Ngóh-deih láih-baai-yih ji láih-baai-ńgh sìh-sìh hòi-wúi.

我 哋 禮 拜 二 至 禮 拜 五 時 時 開 會 。

E. Comparison *(CD 2, Track 61)*

☞ A + adjective + gwo + B
   A + 形容詞 + 過 + B

   eg. Gàm-yaht dung-gwo kàhm-yaht.
   今 日 凍 過 琴 日 。
   (Today is colder than yesterday.)

☞ A + adjective + gwo + B + síu-síu
   A + 形容詞 + 過 + B + 少少

   eg. Gàm-yaht dung-gwo kàhm-yaht síu-síu.
   今 日 凍 過 琴 日 少 少 。
   (Today is a bit colder than yesterday.)

☞ A + adjective + gwo + B + hóu-dò
   A + 形容詞 + 過 + B + 好多

   eg. Gàm-yaht dung-gwo kàhm-yaht hóu-dò.
   今 日 凍 過 琴 日 好 多 。
   (Today is much colder than yesterday.)

1. Yáuh-sìh hàahng-louh faai-gwo daap-chè.
    有 時 行 路 快 過 搭 車 。

2. Ngóh ūk-kéi daaih-gwo néih ūk-kéi.
    我 屋 企 大 過 你 屋 企 。

3. Kàhm-yaht yiht-gwo gàm-yaht síu-síu.
    琴 日 熱 過 今 日 少 少 。

4. Néih-ge Gwóng-dùng-wá (*Cantonese) hóu-gwo kéuih-ge hóu-dò.

你 嘅 廣 東 話 好 過 佢 嘅 好 多 。

5. Nī-gàan jáu-làuh hóu-sihk-gwo gó-gàan.

呢 間 酒 樓 好 食 過 嗰 間 。

6. Kéuih ga chè sàn-gwo Wòhng sàang ge hóu-dò.

佢 架 車 新 過 黃 生 嘅 好 多 。

7. Nī-bún syù gwai-gwo gó-bún síu-síu.

呢 本 書 貴 過 嗰 本 少 少 。

8. Daap dīk-sí syù-fuhk-gwo daap síu-bā.

搭 的 士 舒 服 過 搭 小 巴 。

F. But : 'daahn-haih' 但係 *(CD 2, Track 62)*

1. Ngóh hái Jùng-wàahn fàan-gùng, daahn-haih jyuh hái Jìm-sà-jéui.

我 喺 中 環 返 工 ，但 係 住 喺 尖 沙 咀 。

2. Kàhm-yaht hóu hóu-tìn, daahn-haih gàm-yaht lohk-yúh.

琴 日 好 好 天 ，但 係 今 日 落 雨 。

3. Ngóh kàhm-máahn móuh fan-gaau, daahn-haih yih-gā m̀h-ngáahn-fan.

我 琴 晚 冇 瞓 覺 ，但 係 而 家 唔 眼 瞓 。

4. Ngóh dá dihn-wá béi kéuih, daahn-haih kéuih m̀h-hái ūk-kéi.

我 打 電 話 畀 佢 ，但 係 佢 唔 喺 屋 企 。

5. Chāt-yuht hóu yiht, daahn-haih yāt-yuht hóu dung.

七 月 好 熱 ，但 係 一 月 好 凍 。

6. Chàhn síu-jé móuh sihk-faahn, daahn-haih kéuih m̀h-tóuh-ngoh.

陳 小 姐 冇 食 飯 ， 但 係 佢 唔 肚 餓 。

7. Ūk-kéi hóu yiht, daahn-haih sé-jih-làuh hóu dung.

屋 企 好 熱 ， 但 係 寫 字 樓 好 凍 。

PYRAMID DRILLS *(CD 2, Track 63)*

1.
léuih-hàhng

旅 行

heui léuih-hàhng

去 旅 行

Ngóh heui léuih-hàhng

我 去 旅 行

Ngóh láih-baai-ńgh heui léuih-hàhng

我 禮 拜 五 去 旅 行

Ngóh láih-baai-sàam ji láih-baai-ńgh heui léuih-hàhng.

我 禮 拜 三 至 禮 拜 五 去 旅 行 。

2.
lohk yúh

落 雨

kàhm-yaht lohk yúh

琴 日 落 雨

Gàm-yaht hóu hóu-tìn, kàhm-yaht lohk yúh

今 日 好 好 天 ， 琴 日 落 雨

Gàm-yaht hóu hóu-tìn, daahn-haih kàhm-yaht lohk yúh.

今 日 好 好 天 ， 但 係 琴 日 落 雨 。

3.   daap-chè
                    搭　車

              daap-chè faai
              搭　車　快

        daap-chè faai-gwo hàahng-louh
        搭　車　快　過　行　路

   Daap-chè faai-gwo hàahng-louh hóu-dò.
   搭　車　快　過　行　路　好　多　。

4.   heui Jìm-sà-jéui
                 去　尖　沙　咀

           daap-syùhn heui Jìm-sà-jéui
           搭　船　去　尖　沙　咀

       Néih daap-syùhn heui Jìm-sà-jéui
       你　搭　船　去　尖　沙　咀

     Néih sìh-sìh daap syùhn heui Jìm-sà-jéui.
     你　時　時　搭　船　去　尖　沙　咀　。

SUBSTITUTION DRILLS   *(CD 2, Track 64)*

1. Ngóh sìng-kèih-luhk yáuh-sìh fàan-fùng, yáuh-sìh fong-ga.
    我　星　期　六　有　時　返　工　，　有　時　放　假　。

    a) heui máaih-yéh, hái ūk-kéi 去買嘢，喺屋企
    b) 12:00 fan-gaau, 1:00 fan-gaau 12:00 瞓覺，1:00 瞓覺
    c) heui léuih-hàhng, heui yám-chàh 去旅行，去飲茶

2. Kéuih sìh-sìh tùhng pàhng-yáuh heui yám-chàh.
    佢　時　時　同　朋　友　去　飲　茶　。

a) léuih-hàhng 旅行   *b)* máaih-yéh 買嘢

c) sihk-faahn 食飯

3. Ngóh hóu-síu hái sé-jih-làuh. 我 好 少 喺 寫 字 樓 。

a) tái bou-jí 睇報紙

b) dá dihn-wá béi pàhng-yáuh 打電話畀朋友

c) hái ūk-kéi sihk-faahn 喺屋企食飯

4. Néih ūk-kéi leng-gwo ngóh ūk-kéi hóu-dò.
    你 屋 企 靚 過 我 屋 企 好 多 。

a) daaih 大   *b)* sai 細

c) syù-fuhk 舒服   *d)* yiht 熱

REVIEW EXERCISE

I. Rewrite the following sentences

1. léuih-hàhng / ngóh / jó / heui / luhk-yuht
    旅 行 / 我 / 咗 / 去 / 六 月

2. láih-baai-sàam / nī-go / hòi / sei-dím / wúi
    禮 拜 三 / 呢 個 / 開 / 四 點 / 會

3. hóu / kàhm-yaht / hóu-tìn / a / m̀h
    好 / 琴 日 / 好 天 / 呀 / 唔

4. ngóh / daahn-haih / m̀h-dāk-hàahn / dāk-hàahn / sìng-
    kèih-yih / sìng-kèih-sei
    我 / 但 係 / 唔 得 閒 / 得 閒 / 星 期 二 /
    星 期 四

5. hóu m̀h-hóu / a / heui / ngóh-deih / léuih-hàhng /
    tìng-yaht
    好 唔 好 / 呀 / 去 / 我 哋 / 旅 行 / 聽 日

6. hóu / tìn-hei / ge / gàm-yaht / syù-fuhk
    好 / 天 氣 / 嘅 / 今 日 / 舒 服

II. Translation

1. English books are much more expensive than English newspapers.

2. It didn't rain last week.

3. There is a meeting on Monday, but I'm not free to go.

4. Where will you go next Saturday?

5. It is cold in January. It is hot in July.

6. Sometimes I have lunch with my colleagues, sometimes with my friends.

7. The weather was fine on Friday, but it rained on Saturday.

8. I often have lunch in the office.

9. Are we having a holiday on the 23rd of April?

10. I go to work from Monday to Friday. On Saturday, I go shopping. On Sunday, I sleep at home.

11. It was cloudy last Tuesday.

12. The weather in November is very comfortable.

III. Question and answer *(CD 2, Track 65)*

1. Gàm-yaht haih m̀h-haih yàm-tìn a?
    今 日 係 唔 係 陰 天 呀 ?

2. Néih chāt-yuht fong-m̀h-fong ga a?

你 七 月 放 唔 放 假 呀 ?

3. Hái Hèung-góng, bīn-go-yuht yiht-dī a?

喺 香 港 ， 邊 個 月 熱 啲 呀 ?

4. Néih láih-baai-yaht heui bīn-douh a?

你 禮 拜 日 去 邊 度 呀 ?

5. Lohk-yúh fàan-gùng haih m̀h-haih hóu màh-fàahn a?

落 雨 返 工 係 唔 係 好 麻 煩 呀 ?

6. Bīn-go-yuht ge tìn-hei dung-dī a?

邊 個 月 嘅 天 氣 凍 啲 呀 ?

7. Nī-go yuht ge tìn-hei syù m̀h-syù-fuhk a?

呢 個 月 嘅 天 氣 舒 唔 舒 服 呀 ?

8. Néih jùng-yi heui yám-chàh dò-gwo heui Mahk-dòng-lòuh àh?

你 鍾 意 去 飲 茶 多 過 去 麥 當 勞 吖 ?

9. Néih sìh-sìh daap síu-bā fàan ūk-kéi àh?

你 時 時 搭 小 巴 返 屋 企 吖 ?

LISTENING EXERCISE   *(CD 2, Track 66)*

Listen to the dialogues and answer the questions

1. _____   2. _____   3. _____   4. _____

5. _____   6. _____   7. _____   8. _____

9. _____   10. _____

Lesson 14

Location

A. Asking an office location

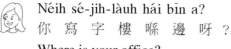

Néih sé-jih-làuh hái bīn a?

你 寫 字 樓 喺 邊 呀 ？

Where is your office?

> bīn 邊 : a contraction
> of 'bīn-douh 邊度'
> (where)

Hái Jùng-wàahn.

喺 中 環 。

It's in Central.

Jùng-wàahn bīn-douh a?

中 環 邊 度 呀 ？

Where in Central?

Sàn-sai-gaai Daaih-hah.

新 世 界 大 廈 。

At the New World Tower.

Káhn m̀h-káhn Ji-deih Gwóng-chèuhng a?

近 唔 近 置 地 廣 場 呀 ？

Is it close to the Landmark?

Hóu káhn. Hái Ji-deih Gwóng-chèuhng deui-mihn.

好 近 。 喺 置 地 廣 場 對 面 。

Very close. It's opposite to the Landmark.

B.   Asking how to go to Wan Chai Market   *(CD 3, Track 2)*

Néih sīk mh-sīk heui Wāan-jái gāai-síh a?

你 識 唔 識 去 灣 仔 街 市 呀 ？

Do you know how to go to Wan Chai Market?

Sīk. Ngóh yáuh-sìh heui gó-douh máaih-yéh.

識 。 我 有 時 去 嗰 度 買 嘢 。

I know. I go there to buy things sometime.

Hái nī-douh daap māt-yéh chè heui Wāan-jái gāai-síh
jeui faai a?

喺 呢 度 搭 乜 嘢 車 去 灣 仔 街 市 最
快 呀 ？

What is the fastest form of transport to go to Wan Chai Market
(form here)?

Daap bā-sí lā. Hái Hahp-wó Jùng-sàm lohk-chè.

搭 巴 士 啦 。 喺 合 和 中 心 落 車 。

You may take a bus and get off at Hopwell Centre.

Néih jì mh-jì géi-dō houh bā-sí heui Hahp-wó Jùng-
sàm a?

你 知 唔 知 幾 多 號 巴 士 去 合 和 中
心 呀 ？

Do you which bus goes to Hopewell Centre?

Daap ńgh-houh, sahp-houh bā-sí lā. Bā-sí-jaahm hái
ngàhn-hòhng chìhn-mihn.

搭 五 號 、 十 號 巴 士 啦 。 巴 士 站 喺
銀 行 前 面 。

You may take bus no. 5 or 10. The bus stop is in front of the
bank.

VOCABULARY   *(CD 3, Track 3)*

1. hauh-mihn 後面 or   PW : back
   hauh-bihn 後便

2. chìhn-mihn 前面 or   PW : in front
   chìhn-bihn 前便

3. seuhng-mihn 上面 or   PW : above; on top of
   seuhng-bihn 上便

4. hah-mihn 下面 or hah-bihn 下便 PW : below; under

5. jó-mihn 左面 or jó-bihn 左便   PW : left side

6. yauh-mihn 右面 or   PW : right side
   yauh-bihn 右便

7. deui-mihn 對面   PW : opposite side

8. fuh-gahn 附近   PW : nearby

9. káhn 近   ADJ : close to

10. chāan-tēng 餐廳 (M: gàan 間)   PW : restaurant

11. gàai-síh 街市 (M: go 個)   PW : market

12. ngàhn-hòhng 銀行 (M: gàan 間) PW : bank

13. pou-táu 舖頭 (M: gàan 間)   PW : shop

14. jáu-dim 酒店 (M: gàan 間)   PW : hotel

15. līp 軬 (M: ga 架 / bouh 部)   N : lift; elevator
    eg. daap līp 搭軬 : take a lift

16. sīk 識   V : know how to; have
                     knowledge of; to
                     know (somebody)

17. yùh-gwó 如果   A : if

18. jauh 就   A : (in case if) ... then

19. síu-síu 少少   ADJ : a little

SENTENCE PATTERNS   *(CD 3, Track 4)*

A. Location

1. Ngóh hái jáu-làuh ge chìhn-mihn daap-chè.

   我 喺 酒 樓 嘅 前 面 搭 車 。

2. Ngóh hái gàai-síh ge hauh-mihn jyuh, máaih-yéh hóu fòng-
   bihn.

   我 喺 街 市 嘅 後 面 住 ， 買 嘢 好 方
   便 。

3. Deih-tit-jaahm ge fuh-gahn yáuh hóu-dò jáu-làuh.

   地 鐵 站 嘅 附 近 有 好 多 酒 樓 。

4. Gó-bún syù hái tói seuhng-mihn.

   嗰 本 書 喺 枱 上 面 。

5. Ngóh jyuh hái néih-ge jó-mihn.

   我 住 喺 你 嘅 左 面 。

6. Kéuih séung heui hah-mihn máaih yéh sihk.

   佢 想 去 下 面 買 嘢 食 。

7. Ngóh-ge sé-jih-làuh hái līp-ge yauh-mihn.

   我 嘅 寫 字 樓 喺 軨 嘅 右 面 。

8. Gó-gàan pou-táu ge deui-mihn yáuh bā-sí-jaahm.

   嗰 間 舖 頭 嘅 對 面 有 巴 士 站 。

B.   Know : 'sīk' 識 *(CD 3, Track 5)*

1. Gó-douh yáuh géi-dō go yàhn a?   Néih sīk m̀h-sīk kéuih-
   deih a?

   嗰 度 有 幾 多 個 人 呀 ？ 你 識 唔 識 佢
   哋 呀 ？

2. Néih sīk m̀h-sīk yìng-màhn a?   Ngóh sīk síu-síu.

   你 識 唔 識 英 文 呀 ？ 我 識 少 少 。

3. Kéuih sīk m̀h-sīk làih ngóh ūk-kéi a?

   佢 識 唔 識 嚟 我 屋 企 呀 ？

4. Ngóh sīk hàahng heui Gām-jūng deih-tit-jaahm.

   我 識 行 去 金 鐘 地 鐵 站 。

5. Ngóh m̀h-sīk tái nī-bún syù.

   我 唔 識 睇 呢 本 書 。

6. Néih sīk m̀h-sīk nī-gàan gūng-sī a?

   你 識 唔 識 呢 間 公 司 呀 ？

7. Kéuih pàhng-yáuh hái Hèung-góng sīk hóu-dò yàhn.

   佢 朋 友 喺 香 港 識 好 多 人 。

8. Ngóh-deih seuhng-go yuht sīk.

   我 哋 上 個 月 識 。

9. Ngóh sīk síu-síu Jùng-màhn (*Chinese language).

   我 識 少 少 中 文 。

10. Ngóh hái Hèung-góng sīk daap-chè, hái Gáu-lùhng m̀h-
    sīk daap-chè.

    我 喺 香 港 識 搭 車 ， 喺 九 龍 唔 識 搭
    車 。

Review on 'sīk' 識 and 'jì' 知 *(CD 3, Track 6)*

☞ sīk + noun / verb

識 + 名詞 / 動詞

☞ jì + statement (of with a question word)

知 + 句 (常含有疑問詞)

1. Ngóh sīk kéuih

   我 識 佢 。

2. Ngóh jì kéuih haih bīn-go.

   我 知 佢 係 邊 個 。

3. Ngóh sīk nī-gàan gūng-sī.

   我 識 呢 間 公 司 。

4. Ngóh jì nī-gàan haih māt-yéh gūng-sī.

   我 知 呢 間 係 乜 嘢 公 司 。

5. Ngóh sīk síu-síu Gwóng-dùng-wá (*Cantonese).

   我 識 少 少 廣 東 話 。

6. Kéuih m̀h-sīk fàan ūk-kéi.

   佢 唔 識 返 屋 企 。

7. Kéuih m̀h-jì daap māt-yéh chè fàan ūk-kéi.

   佢 唔 知 搭 乜 嘢 車 返 屋 企 。

PRACTICE

Translate the following into Cantonese

1. I know that there is a restaurant on the 15th floor.

2. He knows my friend.

3. I don't know where the Hang Seng Bank (*Hàhng-sāng Ngàhn-hòhng 恒生銀行) is.

4. I don't know how to go there.

5. Do you speak English?

6. I can't read Chinese newspapers.

C. If ... then ... : 'yùh-gwó 如果 ... jauh 就' *(CD 3, Track 7)*

1. Néih m̀h-làih jauh dá dihn-wá béi ngóh lā.
   你 唔 嚟 就 打 電 話 畀 我 啦 。

2. Yùh-gwó jùng-yi jauh máaih lā.
   如 果 鍾 意 就 買 啦 。

3. Yùh-gwó dāk-hàahn, jauh yāt-chàih heui sihk-faahn lā.
   如 果 得 閒 ， 就 一 齊 去 食 飯 啦 。

4. Yùh-gwó lohk yúh, fàan-gùng hóu màh-fàahn.
   如 果 落 雨 ， 返 工 好 麻 煩 。

5. Yùh-gwó sìng-kèih-yaht hóu-tìn, ngóh-deih heui bīn-douh wáan a?
   如 果 星 期 日 好 天 ， 我 哋 去 邊 度 玩 呀 ？

PYRAMID DRILLS   *(CD 3, Track 8)*

1.   daap-chè
                      搭　車
            hái chìhn-mihn daap-chè
            喺　前　面　搭　車
         Ngóh hái chìhn-mihn daap-chè
         我　喺　前　面　搭　車
      Ngóh hái jáu-làuh ge chìhn-mihn daap-chè
      我　喺　酒　樓　嘅　前　面　搭　車

2.   sīk Chàhn táai
                      識　陳　太
            Ngóh-deih sīk Chàhn táai
            我　哋　識　陳　太
      Ngóh-deih seuhng-go-yuht sīk-jó Chàhn táai
      我　哋　上　個　月　識　咗　陳　太

3.   dá dihn-wá béi ngóh
                   打　電　話　畀　我
            néih m̀h-heui, dá dihn-wá béi ngóh
            你　唔　去，打　電　話　畀　我
         néih m̀h-heui, jauh dá dihn-wá béi ngóh lā
         你　唔　去，就　打　電　話　畀　我　啦
      Yùh-gwó néih m̀h-heui, jauh dá dihn-wá béi ngóh lā.
      如　果　你　唔　去，就　打　電　話　畀　我　啦。

SUBSTITUTION DRILLS *(CD 3, Track 9)*

1. Néih sīk m̀h-sīk yìng-màhn a?

   你 識 唔 識 英 文 呀 ？

   a) Gwóng-dùng-wá 廣東話

   b) daap-chè fàan ūk-kéi 搭車返屋企

   c) heui deih-tit-jaahm 去地鐵站

   d) tái bou-jí 睇報紙

2. Ngóh jyuh hái néih ge seuhng-mihn.

   我 住 喺 你 嘅 上 面 。

   a) deui-mihn 對面   *b)* hauh-mihn 後面

   c) jó-mihn 左面   *d)* fuh-gahn 附近

3. Hah-bihn yáuh ngàhn-hòhng.

   下 便 有 銀 行 。

   a) sé-jih-làuh 寫字樓   *b)* chāan-tēng 餐廳

   c) jáu-làuh 酒樓   *d)* jáu-dim 酒店

4. Yùh-gwó séung máaih jauh máaih lā.

   如 果 想 買 就 買 啦 。

   a) jùng-yi, sihk dò-dī 鍾意，食多啲

   b) lohk yúh, m̀h-heui léuih-hàhng 落雨，唔去旅行

   c) néih làih, dá dihn-wá béi ngóh 你嚟，打電話畀我

REVIEW EXERCISE

I. Fill in the blanks

1. Ngóh _____ síu-síu Jùng-màhn. Ngóh _____ " 一 ",
   " 二 ", " 三 ", " 十 ", " 人 ".

   我 _____ 少 少 中 文 。 我 _____ " 一 " 、
   " 二 " 、 " 三 " 、 " 十 " 、 " 人 " 。

2. _____ yáuh chín, ngóh _____ máaih chè.

   _____ 有 錢 ， 我 _____ 買 車 。

3. Daap _____ heui Gáu-lùhng hóu syù-fuhk.

   搭 _____ 去 九 龍 好 舒 服 。

4. _____ m̀h-syù-fuhk, _____ fàan ūk-kéi lā.

   _____ 唔 舒 服 ， _____ 返 屋 企 啦 。

5. Yùh-gwó hóu gwuih, ngóh _____ .

   如 果 好 攰 ， 我 _____ 。

6. _____ , ngóh jauh tóuh-ngoh.

   _____ ， 我 就 肚 餓 。

II. Translation

1. My colleague lives nearby.

2. I don't know Mr Wong.

3. If you want to buy English books, go to that shop.

4. I know she is Mrs Lee's friend.

5.   The lift is behind the door.

6.   I'll take a taxi in front of that bank.

7.   There are many good restaurants in Central.

8.   There is a hotel above.

9.   He lives near Causeway Bay.

10.   There is no minibus (passing by) here.

III. Question and answer   *(CD 3, Track 10)*

1.   Néih sīk m̀h-sīk heui daap syùhn a?
你 識 唔 識 去 搭 船 呀 ？

2.   Néih pàhng-yáuh hái bīn-gàan jáu-dim jyuh a?
你 朋 友 喺 邊 間 酒 店 住 呀 ？

3.   Yùh-gwó néih yáuh sahp-maahn-mān, néih máaih māt-yéh a?
如 果 你 有 十 萬 蚊 ， 你 買 乜 嘢 呀 ？

4.   Néih ūk-kéi fuh-gahn yáuh móuh gàai-síh a?   Néih heui m̀h-heui ga?
你 屋 企 附 近 有 冇 街 市 呀 ？ 你 去 唔 去 㗎 ？

5.   Yùh-gwó tìng-yaht hóu-tìn, néih heui bīn-douh wáan a?
如 果 聽 日 好 天 ， 你 去 邊 度 玩 呀 ？

6.   Sái-sáu-gāan (*toilet) hái bīn-bihn a?
洗 手 間 喺 邊 便 呀 ？

7.   Nī-douh fuh-gahn yáuh géi-dō gàan jáu-làuh a?
呢 度 附 近 有 幾 多 間 酒 樓 呀 ？

8. Deih-tit-jaahm yáuh móuh ngàhn-hòhng a? Yáuh māt-
    yéh ngàhn-hòhng a?
    地 鐵 站 有 冇 銀 行 呀 ？ 有 乜 嘢 銀
    行 呀 ？

9. Néih sé-jih-làuh hah-mihn yáuh móuh pou-táu a?
    你 寫 字 樓 下 面 有 冇 舖 頭 呀 ？

10. Néih sīk m̀h-sīk Chàhn sìn-sàang a?
    你 識 唔 識 陳 先 生 呀 ？

IV. Study the map, and answer the questions. *(CD 3, Track 11)*

1. Sé-jih-làuh hái syù-dim (*book store) ge bīn-bihn a?
    寫 字 樓 喺 書 店 嘅 邊 便 呀 ？

2. Bīn-douh yáuh pou-táu a?
    邊 度 有 舖 頭 呀 ？

3. Bīn-douh yáuh baak-fo gūng-sī (*department store) a?
    邊 度 有 百 貨 公 司 呀 ？

4. Gàai-síh hái jáu-làuh ge bīn-bihn a?
    街 市 喺 酒 樓 嘅 邊 便 呀 ？

5.   Sé-jih-làuh ge deui-mihn yáuh móuh jáu-làuh a?
     寫 字 樓 嘅 對 面 有 冇 酒 樓 呀 ?

6.   Chāan-tēng hái bīn-douh a?
     餐 廳 喺 邊 度 呀 ?

7.   Ngóh séung yám-chàh, bīn-douh yáuh jáu-làuh a?
     我 想 飲 茶 ， 邊 度 有 酒 樓 呀 ?

8.   Hái bīn-douh máaih syù a?
     喺 邊 度 買 書 呀 ?

9.   Baak-fo gūng-sī hái chāan-tēng ge bīn-bihn a?
     百 貨 公 司 喺 餐 廳 嘅 邊 便 呀 ?

10. Jáu-dim hái bīn-douh a?
     酒 店 喺 邊 度 呀 ?

11. Jáu-dim ge jó-mihn yáuh móuh syù-dim a?
     酒 店 嘅 左 面 有 冇 書 店 呀 ?

12. Pou-táu hái jáu-làuh ge bīn-bihn a?
     舖 頭 喺 酒 樓 嘅 邊 便 呀 ?

LISTENING EXERCISE   *(CD 3, Track 12)*

Listen to the dialogues and answer the questions

1. _____   2. _____   3. _____

4. _____   5. _____   6. _____

7. _____   8. _____   9. _____

10. _____   11. _____   12. _____

Lesson 15

Learning Cantonese

CONVERSATION   *(CD 3, Track 13)*

A.   Learning Cantonese

Néih jouh-gán māt-yéh a?
你 做 緊 乜 嘢 呀 ？
What are you doing?

Ngóh tái-gán syù.
我 睇 緊 書 。
I am reading a book.

Tái-gán māt-yéh syù a?
睇 緊 乜 嘢 書 呀 ？
What are you reading?

Tái-gán hohk Gwóng-dùng-wá ge syù.
睇 緊 學 廣 東 話 嘅 書 。
I am reading a book on Cantonese.

Néih hohk-gán Gwóng-dùng-wá mē?!
你 學 緊 廣 東 話 咩 ？ ！
Are you learning Chinese?

"mē 咩" indicating the mood of surprise

Haih a.

係 呀 。

Yes.

Hohk-jó géi-noih la?

學 咗 幾 耐 喇 ?

How long have you been learning?

Hohk-jó bun nìhn la.

學 咗 半 年 喇 。

I have studied for half a year.

Gwóng-dùng-wá nàahn m̀h-nàahn a?

廣 東 話 難 唔 難 呀 ?

Do you think Cantonese is difficult?

Hóu nàahn.

好 難 。

It is very difficult.

Néih sīk m̀h-sīk góng a?

你 識 唔 識 講 呀 ?

Can you speak (in Cantonese)?

Ngóh sīk góng síu-síu, daahn-haih hóu séui-pèih.

我 識 講 少 少 ， 但 係 好 水 皮 。

I can speak a little, but very poorly.

B. How long have you been in H.K.? *(CD 3, Track 14)*

Néih làih-jó géi-noih la?

你 嚟 咗 幾 耐 喇 ?

How long have been here?

Yāt nìhn la.
一 年 喇 。
It have been a year.

Néih jùng m̀h-jùng-yi Hèung-góng a?
你 鍾 唔 鍾 意 香 港 呀 ?
Do you like Hong Kong?

Géi jùng-yi.
幾 鍾 意 。
I quite like this place.

Néih wúih hái Hèung-góng jyuh géi-noih a?
你 會 喺 香 港 住 幾 耐 呀 ?
How long will you stay in Hong Kong?

Ńgh nìhn dóu.
五 年 倒 。
Approximately five years.

C. How would you spent your holiday? *(CD 3, Track 15)*

Hah-go láih-baai fong-ga. Néih séung heui bīn-douh wáan a?
下 個 禮 拜 放 假 。 你 想 去 邊 度 玩 呀 ?
There is a holiday next week? Where do you want to go for fun.

Hah-go láih-baai fong-ga mē? Fong māt-yéh ga a?
下 個 禮 拜 放 假 咩 ? 放 乜 嘢 假 呀 ?
There's a holidday next week? What kind of holiday is it?

Haih Gwok-hing.
係 國 慶 。
It's National Day.

Haih àh? Ngóh jàn-haih m̀h-jì. Néih heui bīn-douh wáan a?

係 吖 ？ 我 眞 係 唔 知 。 你 去 邊 度 玩 呀 ？

Really? I did't know about that, where do you go for fun?

Ngóh tùhng ūk-kéi-yàhn heui Sàm-jan.

我 同 屋 企 人 去 深 圳 。

I go to Shenzhen with my family.

> Shenzhen is the city to the north of Hong Kong

Ngóh dōu séung heui Sàm-jan. Yāt-chàih heui hóu m̀h-hóu a?

我 都 想 去 深 圳 。 一 齊 去 好 唔 好 呀 ？

I want to go to Shenzhen too. Shall we go together?

Hóu a. Yāt-jahn sihk-faahn, ngóh-deih kìng-háh lā.

好 呀 。 一 陣 食 飯 ， 我 哋 傾 吓 啦 。

Yes. Let's talk about that at lunch (later)?

VOCABULARY   *(CD 3, Track 16)*

1. nìhn or lìhn 年   TW：year
   * gauh-nín or gauh-lín 舊年, seuhng-nín or seuhng-lín 上年：last year (literally old year)
   * gàm-nín or gàm-lín / gàm-nìhn or gàm-lìhn 今年：this year
   * chēut-nín or chēut-lín 出年, hah-nín or hah-lín 下年：next year (literally the year out)
   * yih-lìhng-lìhng-baat-nìhn 二〇〇八年：Year 2008

2. yaht 日   TW : day

3. jùng-tàuh 鐘頭 (M: go 個)   TW : hour

4. fàn-jùng 分鐘   TW : minute (time spent)

5. géi-noih or géi-loih 幾耐   QW : how long (time spent)

6. noih or loih 耐   ADJ : long time

7. yāt-jahn 一陣   TW : a moment, later

8. pìhng-sìh 平時   TW : usually; normally

9. hohk 學   V : learn

10. góng 講   V : to speak

11. kìng 傾   V : to chat; to discuss

12. nám or lám 諗   V : think

13. wúih 會   AV : will probably, will, shall, may

14. Gwóng-dùng-wá 廣東話   N : Cantonese

SENTENCE PATTERNS   *(CD 3, Track 17)*

A. Action under progress

Affirmative statement :

☞ hái-douh + verb + gán + object

喺度 ＋ 動詞 ＋ 緊 ＋ 名詞

eg. Kéuih hái-douh tái-gán syù.

佢 喺 度 睇 緊 書 。

(He is reading.)

Negative statement :

☞ m̀h-haih + verb + gán + object
唐係 ＋ 動詞 ＋ 緊 ＋ 名詞

eg. Kéuih m̀h-haih tái-gán syù.
佢 唔 係 睇 緊 書 。
(He is not reading.)

Question form :

☞ haih m̀h-haih + verb + gán + object + a?
係唔係 ＋ 動詞 ＋ 緊 ＋ 名詞 ＋ 呀 ？

eg. Kéuih haih m̀h-haih tái-gán syù a?
佢 係 唔 係 睇 緊 書 呀 ？
(Is he reading?)

Answer : Haih. / M̀h-haih.
係 。 / 唔 係 。
(Yes. / No.)

1. Kéuih daap-gán dīk-sí làih nī-douh.
   佢 搭 緊 的 士 嚟 呢 度 。

2. Ngóh sihk-gán faahn, m̀h-séung kìng dihn-wá. Ngóh yāt-
   jahn dá dihn-wá béi néih lā.
   我 食 緊 飯 ， 唔 想 傾 電 話 。 我 一 陣
   打 電 話 畀 你 啦 。

3. Kéuih hái deih-tit-jaahm dáng-gán pàhng-yáuh.
   佢 喺 地 鐵 站 等 緊 朋 友 。

4. Néih hái-douh jouh-gán māt-yéh a?
   你 喺 度 做 緊 乜 嘢 呀 ？

5. Ngóh kàhm-yaht sàam-dím hái jáu-làuh tùhng pàhng-yáuh
    yám-gán chàh.

    我 琴 日 三 點 喺 酒 樓 同 朋 友 飲 緊
    茶 。

6. Kéuih tùhng pàhng-yáuh hái-douh kìng-gán māt-yéh a?

    佢 同 朋 友 喺 度 傾 緊 乜 嘢 呀 ?

7. Ngóh nám-gán fong-jó gùng heui bīn-douh.

    我 諗 緊 放 咗 工 去 邊 度 。

8. Kéuih fàan-gán gùng, m̀h-hái ūk-kéi.

    佢 返 緊 工 ， 唔 喺 屋 企 。

9. Ngóh-deih m̀h-haih góng-gán néih.

    我 哋 唔 係 講 緊 你 。

10. Néih haih m̀h-haih hohk-gán Gwóng-dùng-wá a?

    你 係 唔 係 學 緊 廣 東 話 呀 ?

B. Time spent (Time how long?) *(CD 3, Track 18)*

(I)

sàam fàn-jùng 三分鐘	3 minutes
yāt go jùng-tàuh 一個鐘頭	1 hour
bun go jùng-tàuh 半個鐘頭	0.5 hour
léuhng yaht 兩日	2 days
yāt go láih-baai/ yāt go sìng-kèih 一個禮拜 / 一個星期	1 week
chāt go yuht 七個月	7 months
léuhng nìhn 兩年	2 years

PRACTICE

Read the following terms in Cantonese

1. 4 weeks	6. 5 days	11. 2 hours 20 minutes
2. 36 minutes	7. 8 months	12. 6 hours
3. 9 minutes	8. 30 minutes	13. 4 years
4. 10 days	9. 24 weeks	14. 15 months
5. 7 years	10. 9 weeks	15. 80 days

(II)   *(CD 3, Track 19)*

Time since action completed :

☞ Subject + point of time + place + verb + time spent
主語 ＋ 時間詞 ＋ 地方 ＋ 動詞 ＋ 所需時間

eg. Ngóh kàhm-yaht dáng-jó néih yāt go jùng-tàuh.
我 琴 日 等 咗 你 一 個 鐘 頭 。
(I waited for you an hour yesterday.)

Duration of action :

☞ Subject + point of time + place + verb + (jó) +
time spent + object
主語 ＋ 時間詞 ＋ 地方 ＋ 動詞 ＋ （咗） ＋
所需時間 ＋ 名詞

eg. Ngóh kàhm yaht sihk-jó sahp-ńgh fàn-jùng
jóu-chāan.
我 琴 日 食 咗 十 五 分 鐘 早
餐 。
(I spent 15 minutes to have breakfast yesterday.)

Question form :

☞ verb + (yiu) géi-noih a?
動詞 + （要）幾耐呀？

   eg. Nī-douh heui Tùhng-lòh-wāan yiu géi-noih a?
     呢 度 去 銅 鑼 灣 要 幾 耐 呀 ？
     (How long does it takes to go to Causeway Bay?)

1. Kéuih làih-jó léuhng go láih-baai.
   佢 嚟 咗 兩 個 禮 拜 。

2. Ngóh heui gó-douh sahp yih yaht.
   我 去 嗰 度 十 二 日 。

3. Kéuih gàm-yaht hái Jùng-wàahn hàahng-jó (*walk) hóu noih.
   佢 今 日 喺 中 環 行 咗 好 耐 。

4. Ngóh tùhng kéuih kìng-jó yāt-jahn dihn-wá.
   我 同 佢 傾 咗 一 陣 電 話 。

5. Néih daap-jó géi-noih chè làih a?
   你 搭 咗 幾 耐 車 嚟 呀 ？

6. Néih hàahng-louh fàan ūk-kéi yiu géi-noih a?
   你 行 路 返 屋 企 要 幾 耐 呀 ？

7. Kéuih hái nī-gàan gūng-sī jouh-jó (*work) sàam nìhn.
   佢 喺 呢 間 公 司 做 咗 三 年 。

8. Ngóh hohk-jó Gwóng-dùng-wá bun nìhn la.
   我 學 咗 廣 東 話 半 年 喇 。

9. Néih nám-jó géi-noih a? Ngóh nám-jó léuhng yaht.
   你 諗 咗 幾 耐 呀 ？ 我 諗 咗 兩 日 。

10. Nī-bún syù máaih-jó géi-noih la?

呢 本 書 買 咗 幾 耐 喇 ?

11. Kéuih hái Wāan-jái jyuh-jó sei go yuht la.

佢 喺 灣 仔 住 咗 四 個 月 喇 。

12. Néih làih-jó Hèung-góng géi-noih a?

你 嚟 咗 香 港 幾 耐 呀 ?

C.   Will probably, will : 'wúih' 會 *(CD 3, Track 20)*

1. Néih cheut-nín wúih heui bīn-douh léuih-hàhng a?

你 出 年 會 去 邊 度 旅 行 呀 ?

2. Néih taai-táai géi-sìh wúih làih Hèung-góng a?

你 太 太 幾 時 會 嚟 香 港 呀 ?

3. Ngóh chāt-yuht wúih fong-ga.

我 七 月 會 放 假 。

4. Tìng-yaht wúih m̀h-wúih hóu-tìn a?

聽 日 會 唔 會 好 天 呀 ?

5. Ngóh m̀h-wúih dá dihn-wá béi kéuih.

我 唔 會 打 電 話 畀 佢 。

6. Néih wúih m̀h-wúih tái nī-fahn bou-jí a?

你 會 唔 會 睇 呢 份 報 紙 呀 ?

7. Ngóh wúih máaih gó-jì bāt.

我 會 買 嗰 枝 筆 。

8. Ngóh dāk-hàahn wúih tùhng pàhng-yáuh yám-chàh.

我 得 閒 會 同 朋 友 飲 茶 。

PYRAMID DRILLS *(CD 3, Track 21)*

1.
       māt-yéh a?
       乜　嘢　呀？

      kìng māt-yéh a?
      傾　乜　嘢　呀？

     kìng-gán māt-yéh a?
     傾　緊　乜　嘢　呀？

   hái douh kìng-gán māt-yéh a?
   喺　度　傾　緊　乜　嘢　呀？

 Kéuih hái douh kìng-gán māt-yéh a?
 佢　喺　度　傾　緊　乜　嘢　呀？

Kéuih tùhng pàhng-yáuh hái douh kìng-gán māt-yéh a?
佢　同　朋　友　喺　度　傾　緊　乜　嘢　呀？

2.
       hóu-tìn
       好　天

      wúih hóu-tìn
      會　好　天

    m̀h-wúih hóu-tìn
    唔　會　好　天

  wúih m̀h-wúih hóu-tìn
  會　唔　會　好　天

Tìng-yaht wúih m̀h-wúih hóu-tìn a?
聽　日　會　唔　會　好　天　呀？

3.　　　　　　léuhng go jùng-tàuh
　　　　　　　兩　個　鐘　頭
　　　　　dáng-jó néih léuhng go jùng-tàuh
　　　　　等　咗　你　兩　個　鐘　頭
　　hái chāan-tèng dáng-jó néih léuhng go jùng-tàuh
　　喺　餐　廳　等　咗　你　兩　個　鐘　頭
　Ngóh hái chāan-tèng dáng-jó néih léuhng go jùng-tàuh.
　我　喺　餐　廳　等　咗　你　兩　個　鐘　頭。
Ngóh sìng-kèih-yāt hái chāan-tèng dáng-jó néih léuhng go jùng-tàuh.
我　星　期　一　喺　餐　廳　等　咗　你　兩　個　鐘　頭。

SUBSTITUTION DRILLS　*(CD 3, Track 22)*

1.　Ngóh làih-jó Hèung-góng léuhng-go láih-baai.
　　我　嚟　咗　香　港　兩　個　禮　拜。

　　a) sei nìhn 四年

　　b) gáu go yuht 九個月

　　c) yih sahp ńgh yaht 二十五日

　　d) chāt go sìng-kèih 七個星期

2.　Ngóh hái jáu-dim sihk-gán aan.
　　我　喺　酒　店　食　緊　晏。

　　a) yám chàh 飲茶　　　　　*b)* dáng pàhng-yáuh 等朋友

　　c) fàan gùng 返工

3. Kéuih baat-yuht m̀h-wúih <u>fong-ga.</u>

    佢 八 月 唔 會 放 假 。

    a) heui léuih-hàhng 去旅行   b) hòi-wúi 開會

    c) làih Hèung-góng 嚟香港

REVIEW EXERCISE

I.   Translation

1. My friends will learn Cantonese.

2. What are you doing?

3. I'm working. I'll call you in a moment.

4. How long have you been waiting for me?

5. I've been here for 3 years.

6. Who are you talking to?

7. How long does it take you to have lunch?

8. How long ago did you buy this TV set?

9. Usually when you have free time, what will you do?

10. I thought about that for one minute.

11. Will it rain on Friday?

12. I will go to Tsim Sha Tsui shopping on Sunday. Are you coming?

II. Question and answer   *(CD 3, Track 23)*

1. Néih dāk-hàahn jouh māt-yéh a ?
   你 得 閒 做 乜 嘢 呀 ?

2. Néih sìng-kèih-luhk wúih heui bīn-douh a?
   你 星 期 六 會 去 邊 度 呀 ?

3. Néih pìhng-sìh dáng pàhng-yáuh, dáng géi-noih a?
   你 平 時 等 朋 友 , 等 幾 耐 呀 ?

4. Néih gàm-máahn wúih m̀h-wúih dá dihn-wá béi ngóh a?
   你 今 晚 會 唔 會 打 電 話 畀 我 呀 ?

5. Néih pìhng-sìh yāt-dím jouh-gán māt-yéh a?
   你 平 時 一 點 做 緊 乜 嘢 呀 ?

6. Néih hohk-gán Gwóng-dùng-wá àh? Hohk-jó gèi-
   noih a?
   你 學 緊 廣 東 話 吖 ? 學 咗 幾 耐 呀 ?

7. Néih pìhng-sìh daap-chè fàan-gùng yiu géi-noih a?
   你 平 時 搭 車 返 工 要 幾 耐 呀 ?

8. Kéuih góng-gán dihn-wá àh?
   佢 講 緊 電 話 吖 ?

9. Nī-douh heui Jùng-wàahn yiu géi-noih a? Daap māt-
   yéh chè jeui (*most) faai a?
   呢 度 去 中 環 要 幾 耐 呀 ? 搭 乜 嘢
   車 最 快 呀 ?

10. Néih hái Hèung-góng jyuh-jó géi-noih la?
    你 喺 香 港 住 咗 幾 耐 喇 ?

III. Review on 'yih' 二 and 'léuhng' 兩

1. 2 years	9. 22 people
2. 2:10	10. Year 2002
3. 2nd of January	11. $2
4. 2 hours 20 minutes	12. 2,000 sheets of paper
5. $2.20	13. 2/2/1992
6. Tuesday	14. 202 minutes
7. February	15. 212 months
8. $0.20	16. 200 weeks

Lesson 16

Tour Around Hong Kong

CONVERSATION *(CD 3, Track 24)*

A. Chinese food in Hong Kong

Néih heui-gwo Sài-gung sihk hói-sìn meih a?

你 去 過 西 貢 食 海 鮮 未 呀 ？

Have you been to Sai Kung to eat seafood?

Heui-gwo. Ngóh tùhng Hèung-góng pàhng-yáuh heui sihk-gwo géi chi la.

去 過 。 我 同 香 港 朋 友 去 食 過 幾 次 喇 。

Yes. I've been there with my Hong Kong friends a few times.

Néih jùng m̀h-jùng-yi sihk a?

你 鍾 唔 鍾 意 食 呀 ？

Do you like it?

Hóu jùng-yi. Hèung-góng ge hói-sìn hóu hóu-sihk. Ngóh dōu hóu jùng-yi heui yám-chàh.

好 鍾 意 。 香 港 嘅 海 鮮 好 好 食 。 我 都 好 鍾 意 去 飲 茶 。

Yes. The seafood in Hong Kong is very tasty. I also like to go for dim sum.

Néih jeui jùng-yi sihk māt-yéh dím-sām a?

你 最 鍾 意 食 乜 嘢 點 心 呀 ?

What is your favourite dim sum?

Ngóh jeui jùng-yi sihk há-gáau tùhng chā-sīu-bāau.

我 最 鍾 意 食 蝦 餃 同 叉 燒 飽 。

I like shrimp dumpling and BBQ pork bun the most.

B. Have your family ever been to Hong Kong? *(CD 3, Track 25)*

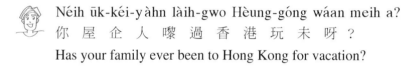

Néih ūk-kéi-yàhn làih-gwo Hèung-góng wáan meih a?

你 屋 企 人 嚟 過 香 港 玩 未 呀 ?

Has your family ever been to Hong Kong for vacation?

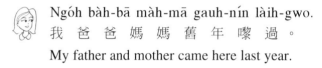

Ngóh bàh-bā màh-mā gauh-nín làih-gwo.

我 爸 爸 媽 媽 舊 年 嚟 過 。

My father and mother came here last year.

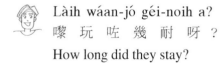

Làih wáan-jó géi-noih a?

嚟 玩 咗 幾 耐 呀 ?

How long did they stay?

Làih-jó yāt go yuht dóu.

嚟 咗 一 個 月 倒 。

Approximately one month.

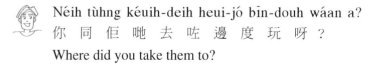

Néih tùhng kéuih-deih heui-jó bīn-douh wáan a?

你 同 佢 哋 去 咗 邊 度 玩 呀 ?

Where did you take them to?

Heui-jó Chek-chyúh, Chín-séui Wāan, tùhng-màaih heui-jó Tùhng-lòh-wāan máaih-yéh.

去 咗 赤 柱 、 淺 水 灣 ， 同 埋 去 咗 銅 鑼 灣 買 嘢 。

We went to Stanley, Repulse Bay, and shopping in Causeway Bay.

Kéuih-deih hòi m̀h-hòi-sàm a?

佢 哋 開 唔 開 心 呀 ？

Did they have fun?

Kéuih-deih hóu hòi-sàm. Juhng wah hóu hóu-wáan tìm.

佢 哋 好 開 心 。 仲 話 好 好 玩 喺 。

They were happy, and they said they enjoyed it so much.

C.   Going to see a movie   *(CD 3, Track 26)*

Néih tái-gwo Hèung-góng ge hei meih a?

你 睇 過 香 港 嘅 戲 未 呀 ？

Have you ever seen any Hong Kong films?

Meih tái-gwo.

未 睇 過 。

No, I haven't.

Yìh-gā yáuh tou hóu hóu-tái ge hei. Ngóh-deih yāt-chàih heui tái, hóu m̀h-hóu a?

而 家 有 套 好 好 睇 嘅 戲 。 我 哋 一 齊 去 睇 ， 好 唔 好 呀 ？

There is a very good movie on show, shall we go to see it?

Hóu, ngóh hóu séung tái. Ngóh-deih géi-sìh heui tái a?

好 ， 我 好 想 睇 。 我 哋 幾 時 去 睇
呀 ？

Yes, I really want to see it. When shall we go?

Néih tìng-máahn dāk m̀h-dāk-hàahn a?

你 聽 晚 得 唔 得 閒 呀 ？

Are you free tomorrow evening?

Dāk-hàahn. Ngóh-deih tìng-máahn heui tái lā.

得 閒 。 我 哋 聽 晚 去 睇 啦 。

Yes. Let's go to see it tomorrow evening.

Hóu a. Néih luhk-dím jáu-dāk meih a?

好 呀 。 你 六 點 走 得 未 呀 ？

OK. Can you leave the office at 6:00?

Ngóh luhk-dím meih jáu-dāk. Luhk-dím-bun lā, hóu m̀h-hóu a?

我 六 點 未 走 得 。 六 點 半 啦 ， 好 唔
好 呀 ？

I can't leave at 6:00. What about 6:30?

Hóu. Ngóh-deih heui sihk-faahn sìn, jì-hauh heui tái hei lā.

好 。 我 哋 去 食 飯 先 ， 之 後 去 睇 戲
啦 。

OK. We will have dinner first, and then go to the movie.

VOCABULARY   *(CD 3, Track 27)*

1. chi 次   N : occasion, times
2. verb + gwo 過   VS : indicating experiences
3. meih 未   P : not yet
4. verb + dāk 得   V/VS : allow to, can, O.K.
5. sìn 先   A : first
6. jì-hauh 之後   TW : afterwards; later on
7. tái hei 睇戲   VO : see a movie
   * hei 戲 (M: tou 套) : movie
8. gin 見   V : meet
9. Yaht-bún choi 日本菜   N : Japanese food
   * Jùng-gwok choi 中國菜 : Chinese food
   * Taai-gwok choi 泰國菜 : Thai food
   * Yuht-nàahm choi 越南菜 : Vietnamese food
   * Hòhn-gwok choi 韓國菜 : Korean food
   * Yi-daaih-leih choi 意大利菜 : Italian food
   * Faat-gwok choi 法國菜 : French food
10. tèng 聽   V : listen; hear
11. chéng 請   V : invite; treat
12. jáu 走   V : leave
13. laaht 辣   ADJ : hot and spicy
    * tìhm 甜 : sweet
    * hàahm 鹹 : salty
    * syùn 酸 : sour
    * fú 苦 : bitter

SENTENCE PATTERNS *(CD 3, Track 28)*

A. Showing one's experience

Affirmative statement :

☞ verb + gwo
動詞 + 過

eg. Néih heui-gwo ngóh ūk-kéi.
你 去 過 我 屋 企 。
(You've been to my house.)

Negative statement :

☞ móuh + verb + gwo
冇 + 動詞 + 過

eg. Néih móuh heui-gwo ngóh ūk-kéi.
你 冇 去 過 我 屋 企 。
(You've never been to my house.)

Question form :

☞ yáuh móuh + verb + gwo + object + a?
有冇 + 動詞 + 動詞 + 過 + 名詞 + 呀 ?

eg. Néih yáuh móuh heui-gwo ngóh ūk-kéi a?
你 有 冇 去 過 我 屋 企 呀 ?
(Have you ever been to my house?)

Answer : Yáuh. / Móuh.
有 。 / 冇 。
(Yes. / No.)

1. Néih yáuh móuh heui-gwo gó-douh yám-chàh a?
   你 有 冇 去 過 嗰 度 飲 茶 呀 ？

2. Ngóh-deih sihk-gwo Yaht-bún choi géi chi.
   我 哋 食 過 日 本 菜 幾 次 。

3. Kéuih gauh-nín làih-gwo Hèung-góng.
   佢 舊 年 嚟 過 香 港 。

4. Ngóh gàm-yaht móuh yám-gwo chàh.
   我 今 日 冇 飲 過 茶 。

5. Kéuih pàhng-yáuh móuh làih-gwo Hèung-góng.
   佢 朋 友 冇 嚟 過 香 港 。

6. Néih yáuh móuh heui-gwo Chín-séui-wāan (*Repulse Bay) a?
   你 有 冇 去 過 淺 水 灣 呀 ？

7. Ngóh sīk síu-síu Gwóng-dùng-wá, daahn-haih ngóh móuh hohk-gwo.
   我 識 少 少 廣 東 話 ， 但 係 我 冇 學 過 。

8. Seuhng-go láih-baai yáuh móuh hòi-gwo wúi a?
   上 個 禮 拜 有 冇 開 過 會 呀 ？

9. Ngóh kàhm-máahn móuh fan-gwo gaau.
   我 琴 晚 冇 瞓 過 覺 。

10. Ngóh daap-gwo síu-bā làih nī-douh, daahn-haih móuh daap-gwo bā-sí làih.
    我 搭 過 小 巴 嚟 呢 度 ， 但 係 冇 搭 過 巴 士 嚟 。

B.   Not yet : 'meih' 未   *(CD 3, Track 29)*

Negative statement :

☞   meih + verb + (gwo)

未 + 動詞 + （過）

eg. Néih meih heui ngóh ūk-kéi.

你 未 去 我 屋 企 。

(You haven't gone to my house yet.)

Néih meih heui-gwo ngóh ūk-kéi.

你 未 去 過 我 屋 企 。

(You've never been to my house.)

Question form :

☞   verb (jó / gwo) + object + meih a?

動詞 （咗 / 過） + 名詞 + 未呀 ？

eg. Néih heui-jó ngóh ūk-kéi meih a?

你 去 咗 我 屋 企 未 呀 ？

(Have you gone to my house?)

Answer :   Heui-jó la. / Meih heui.

去 咗 喇 。 / 未 去 。

(Yes. / No.)

Néih heui-gwo ngóh ūk-kéi meih a?

你 去 過 我 屋 企 未 呀 ？

(Have you ever been to my house?)

Answer :   Heui-gwo la. / Meih heui-gwo.

去 過 喇 。 / 未 去 過 。

(Yes. / No.)

1. Néih gin-gwo Wòhng sàang meih a?

    你 見 過 黃 生 未 呀 ？

2. Ngóh m̀h-dāk-hàahn, só-yíh (*therefore) meih dá dihn-wá béi kéuih.

    我 唔 得 閒 ， 所 以 未 打 電 話 畀 佢 。

3. Kéuih gàm-yaht meih sihk-gwo yéh.

    佢 今 日 未 食 過 嘢 。

4. Sihk-jó faahn meih a?

    食 咗 飯 未 呀 ？

5. Léih síu-jé meih daap-gwo deih-tit.

    李 小 姐 未 搭 過 地 鐵 。

6. Ngóh gin-gwo kéuih, meih gin-gwo kéuih taai-táai.

    我 見 過 佢 ， 未 見 過 佢 太 太 。

7. Néih-deih hòi-jó wúi meih a?

    你 哋 開 咗 會 未 呀 ？

8. Kéuih meih hohk-gwo Gwóng-dùng-wá, kéuih séung hohk Gwóng-dùng-wá.

    佢 未 學 過 廣 東 話 ， 佢 想 學 廣 東 話 。

9. Kéuih meih làih, ngóh-deih dáng m̀h-dáng kéuih a?

    佢 未 嚟 ， 我 哋 等 唔 等 佢 呀 ？

C. Can or allow to : 'dāk' 得 *(CD 3, Track 30)*

Affirmative statement :

☞   verb + dāk

      動詞 + 得

eg. Kéuih làih-dāk.

佢 嚟 得 。

(He can come.)

Negative statement :

☞ m̀h + verb + dāk

唔 + 動詞 + 得

eg. Kéuih m̀h-làih-dāk.

佢 唔 嚟 得 。

(He can't come.)

Question form :

☞ verb + m̀h + verb + dāk + a?

動詞 + 唔 + 動詞 + 得 + 呀 ?

eg. Kéuih làih m̀h-làih dāk a?

佢 嚟 唔 嚟 得 呀 ?

(Can he come?)

☞ statement + dāk m̀h-dāk a?

句 + 得 唔 得 呀 ?

eg. Ngóh yìh-gā làih, dāk m̀h-dāk a?

我 而 家 嚟 ， 得 唔 得 呀 ?

(May I come now?)

Answer : Dāk. / M̀h-dāk

得 。 / 唔 得 。

(Yes. / No.)

1. Ngóh tìng-yaht m̀h-dāk-hàahn, m̀h-heui-dāk yám-chàh.

我 聽 日 唔 得 閒 ， 唔 去 得 飲 茶 。

2. Ngóh m̀h-sihk-dāk laaht (ge yéh).
   我 唔 食 得 辣 （嘅 嘢）。

3. Néih yáuh hóu-dò yéh yiu jouh, néih meih jáu-dāk.
   你 有 好 多 嘢 要 做 ， 你 未 走 得 。

4. Nī-douh m̀h-jyun-dāk yauh.
   呢 度 唔 轉 得 右 。

5. Ngóh hóu gwuih, m̀h-hàahng-dāk la.
   我 好 劫 ， 唔 行 得 喇 。

6. Nī-dī yéh sihk m̀h-sihk-dāk ga?
   呢 啲 嘢 食 唔 食 得 㗎 ？

7. Ngóh m̀h-sīk-dāk kéuih. Kéuih haih bīn-go a? Ngóh-deih gin-gwo kéuih meih ga?
   我 唔 識 得 佢 。 佢 係 邊 個 呀 ？ 我 哋
   見 過 佢 未 㗎 ？

8. Chàhn sìn-sàang gàm-yaht m̀h-fàan-dāk gùng.
   陳 先 生 今 日 唔 返 得 工 。

9. Ngóh m̀h-daap-dāk syùhn.
   我 唔 搭 得 船 。

10. Ngóh jáu sìn, dāk m̀h-dāk a?
    我 走 先 ， 得 唔 得 呀 ？

11. Pèhng-dī dāk m̀h-dāk a?
    平 啲 得 唔 得 呀 ？

12. Néih chéng ngóh sihk-faahn, dāk m̀h-dāk a?
    你 請 我 食 飯 ， 得 唔 得 呀 ？

D. First : 'sìn' 先 *(CD 3, Track 31)*

1. M̀h-gòi heui Wāan-jái sìn, jì-hauh heui Tùhng-lòh-wāan.
    唐 該 去 灣 仔 先 ，之 後 去 銅 鑼 灣 。

2. Néih-deih sihk sìn lā.
    你 哋 食 先 啦 。

3. Néih hàahng sìn lā.
    你 行 先 啦 。

4. Ngóh jáu sìn la. Tìng-yaht gin.
    我 走 先 喇 。 聽 日 見 。

5. Néih tóuh-ngoh jauh sihk-faahn sìn lā.
    你 肚 餓 就 食 飯 先 啦 。

6. Néih dáng ngóh yāt-jahn, ngóh yiu tèng dihn-wá sìn.
    你 等 我 一 陣 ，我 要 聽 電 話 先 。

7. Néih-deih hàahng sìn. Ngóh chìh-dī làih.
    你 哋 行 先 。 我 遲 啲 嚟 。

PYRAMID DRILLS   *(CD 3, Track 32)*

1.
                    Gwóng-dùng-wá
                    廣 東 話
                hohk Gwóng-dùung-wá
                學 廣 東 話
            hohk-gwo Gwóng-dùng-wá
            學 過 廣 東 話
        móuh hohk-gwo Gwóng-dùng-wá
        冇 學 過 廣 東 話

yáuh móuh hohk-gwo Gwóng-dùng-wá a?

有 冇 學 過 廣 東 話 呀？

Néih yáuh móuh hohk-gwo Gwóng-dùng-wá a?

你 有 冇 學 過 廣 東 話 呀？

2. Léih síu-jé

李 小 姐

gin Léih síu-jé

見 李 小 姐

gin-gwo Léih síu-jé

見 過 李 小 姐

meih gin-gwo Léih síu-jé

未 見 過 李 小 姐

Ngóh meih gin-gwo Léih síu-jé.

我 未 見 過 李 小 姐。

3. dá dihn-wá

打 電 話

dá dihn-wá béi néih

打 電 話 畀 你

dá-jó dihn-wá béi néih

打 咗 電 話 畀 你

Chàhn táai dá-jó dihn-wá béi néih

陳 太 打 咗 電 話 畀 你

Chàhn táai dá-jó dihn-wá béi néih meih a?

陳 太 打 咗 電 話 畀 你 未 呀？

4. m̀h-fàan-gùng

唔 返 工

m̀h-fàan-dāk gùng

唐　返　得　工

gàm-yaht m̀h-fàan-dāk gùng

今　日　唐　返　得　工

Wóhng sìn-sàang gàm-yaht m̀h-fàan-dāk gùng

王　先　生　今　日　唐　返　得　工

Wóhng sìn-sàang gàm-yaht fàan m̀h-fàan-dāk gùng a?

王　先　生　今　日　返　唐　返　得　工　呀？

SUBSTITUTION DRILLS   *(CD 3, Track 33)*

1. Nī-dī dím-sām hóu tìhm.

   呢　的　點　心　好　甜　。

   a) hàahm 鹹   *b)* laaht 辣

   c) yiht 熱   *d)* syùn 酸

2. Ngóh meih heui-gwo yám-chàh.

   我　未　去　過　飲　茶　。

   a) hòi wúi 開會

   b) Chín-séui-wāan 淺水灣

   c) sihk Yi-daaih-leih choi 食意大利菜

3. Kéuih gàm-yaht m̀h-dāk-hàahn, kéuih m̀h-heui-dāk yám chàh.

   佢　今　日　唐　得　閒，佢　唐　去　得　飲　茶　。

   a) làih-dāk hòi wúi 嚟得開會

   b) fàan-dāk ūk-kéi sihk faahn 返得屋企食飯

   c) tái-dāk dihn-sih 睇得電視

4. M̀h-gòi néih heui Tùhng-lòh-wāan sìn.

    唔　該　你　去　銅　鑼　灣　先　。

    a) yám tòng 飲湯

    b) máaih syù 買書

    c) dá dihn-wá béi kéuih 打電話畀佢

    d) fàan gūng-sī 返公司

REVIEW EXERCISE

I.   Translation

1. Have you ever been to that restaurant to eat dim sum?

2. I remember but I have not done it yet.

3. Have you ever been to Central by MTR?

4. I have never been to your house.

5. He is sick. He cannot attend the meeting today.

6. Is this sweet or salty?

7. You eat first. I'm not hungry.

8. I have to answer the phone first. We'll talk later.

9. You cannot go straight here. You have to turn left.

10. I have never met him before. Who is he?

11. She has not come back yet.

12. Did you see that movie? I've seen it twice.

II. Question and answer *(CD 3, Track 34)*

1. Néih yáuh móuh hái Sùhng-gwòng (*Sogo) máaih-
   gwo yéh a?

   你 有 冇 喺 崇 光 買 過 嘢 呀 ?

2. Néih yám-gwo lèuhng-chàh (*Chinese herbal tea) meih
   a?

   你 飲 過 涼 茶 未 呀 ?

3. Néih sihk-gwo Yi-daaih-leih choi meih a? Heui-gwo
   'Pizza Hut' meih a?

   你 食 過 意 大 利 菜 未 呀 ? 去 過
   'Pizza Hut' 未 呀 ?

4. Néih chéng ngóh heui yám-chàh dāk m̀h-dāk a? Néih
   géi-sìh dāk-hàahn a?

   你 請 我 去 飲 茶 得 唔 得 呀 ? 你 幾
   時 得 閒 呀 ?

5. Néih yáuh móuh heui-gwo Nàahm-ā Dóu (*Lamma
   Island) sihk hói-sìn a?

   你 有 冇 去 過 南 丫 島 食 海 鮮 呀 ?

6. Néih heui-gwo kéuih ūk-kéi meih a?

   你 去 過 佢 屋 企 未 呀 ?

7. Sihk-jó faahn meih a? Sihk-jó géi-noih la?

   食 咗 飯 未 呀 ? 食 咗 幾 耐 喇 ?

8. Pìhng-sìh néih dihng néih taai-táai fàan ūk-kéi sìn a?

   平 時 你 定 你 太 太 返 屋 企 先 呀 ?

9. Néih yáuh móuh hái Chín-séui-wāan (*Repulse Bay) jyuh-gwo a?

你 有 冇 喺 淺 水 灣 住 過 呀 ？

10. Néih gáu-dím hái-douh meih a?

你 九 點 喺 度 未 呀 ？

Appendix 1

Cantonese to English

Lesson

A

aan 晏	7	N :	lunch

B

bā-sí 巴士 (M: ga 架)	3	N :	bus
baahk-sīk 白色	6	N :	white
bāai-baai 拜拜	2		goodbye
baak 百	10	NU :	hundred
baak-fo gūng-sī 百貨公司	14	PW :	department store
baat 八	1	NU :	eight
báau 飽	8	ADJ :	full (stomach)
bāt 筆 (M: jì 枝)	9	N :	pen
bē-jáu 啤酒	11	N :	beer
béi 畀	11	V :	give
bīn-douh 邊度	3	QW :	where
bīn-go 邊個	5	QW :	which one; who
bīn-go yuht 邊個月	13	QW :	which month
bou-jí 報紙 (M: fahn 份)	11	N :	newspaper

būi 杯 (M: jek 隻 / go 個)   9   N :   cup; glass; mug

C

chà-sìu-bāau 叉燒包   10   N :   BBQ pork bun

chà-sìu faahn 叉燒飯   9   N :   BBQ pork with rice

chāan-tēng 餐廳   14   PW :   restaurant
(M: gàan 間)

cháang-sīk 橙色   6   N :   orange colour

chāt 七   1   N :   seven

Chek-chyúh 赤柱   16   PW :   Stanley

chéng 請   16   V :   invite; treat

chéng-mahn 請問   11   PH :   may I ask?

chēut-nín 出年   15   TW :   next year

chi 次   16   N :   measuring occasion

chìhn-mihn 前面   14   N :   front

chìn 千   10   NU :   thousand

chìh-dī dá làih 遲啲打嚟   5   call later

chìh-dou 遲到   2   late

chìh-gāng 匙羹 (M: jek 隻)   11   N :   spoon

Chín-séui-wāan 淺水灣   16   PW :   Repulse Bay

choi 菜   11   N :   vegetables

D

dá cho 打錯   5   dialed   the   wrong   number

dá dihn-wá 打電話   5   VO :   make telephone call

daaih 大	6	ADJ :	big; large
dāan 單 (M: jèung 張)	11	N :	receipt; bill; invoice
daahn-haih 但係	13	ADV :	but; however
daap chè 搭車	8	VO :	take a car, bus, etc.
daap līp 搭軨	14	VO :	take a lift
dāk 得	6/16	V/VS :	O.K.; allow to; can
dāk-hàahn 得閒	8	ADJ :	have free time
dang 凳 (M: jèung 張)	11	N :	chair
Dáng ngóh làih gaai-siuh 等我嚟介紹	4		Let me introduce
dāng-wái 燈位 (M: go 個)	3	N :	traffic lights
dehng tói 訂枱	12	VO :	reserve table
deih-há 地下	12	PW :	ground floor
deih-tit 地鐵 (M: ga 架)	3	N :	MTR
deih-tit-jaahm 地鐵站	3	PW :	MTR station
deui-mihn 對面	14	PW :	opposite (side)
dī 啲 + N	4	M :	indicating plural form or uncountable
ADJ + dī 啲	6	ADV	a little more
dihn-wá 電話 (M: go 個)	5	N :	telephone
dihng-haih 定係	9	CON :	or (in a question)
dīk-sí 的士 (M: ga 架)	3	N :	taxi
dím 點	7	TW :	o'clock
dím-gáai 點解	8	QW :	why
dím-sām 點心 (M: go 個)	10	N :	dim sum
dò-jeh 多謝	2		thank you

dōu 都	10	ADV :	also
N + dóu 倒	15	P :	approximately
douh 度	13	N :	degree
dung 凍	9	ADJ :	cold
dung séui 凍水	10	N :	cold water

F

faahn 飯	10	N :	rice
faai 快	13	ADJ :	fast; quick
faai-jí 筷子	11	N :	chopsticks
fàan-gùng 返工	7	VO :	go to work
fàan ūk-kéi 返屋企	7	VO :	go home
fan-gaau 瞓覺	7	VO :	sleep
fán-hùhng-sīk 粉紅色	6	N :	pink
fàn-jùng 分鐘	15	TW :	minute (time spent)
fòng-bihn 方便	12	ADJ :	convenient
fong-ga 放假	13	VO :	on holiday
fú 苦	16	ADJ :	bitter
fuh-gahn 附近	14	PW :	nearby
fùi-sīk 灰色	6	N :	grey
fun-yìhng gwòng làhm 歡迎光臨	11		welcome

G

ga-fē 咖啡	9	N :	coffee
(ga-)fē-sīk （咖）啡色	6	N :	brown

gàai-háu 街口 (M: go 個)   3   PW :   street corner

gàai-síh 街市 (M: go 個)   14   PW :   market

gám 咁   12   P :   well

gàm-go láih-baai 今個禮拜   13   TW :   this week

gàm-go yuht 今個月   13   TW :   this month

Gām-jūng 金鐘   12   PW :   Admiralty

gàm-nín 今年   15   TW :   this year

gàm-sīk 金色   6   N :   gold

gàm-yaht 今日   10   TW :   today

gáu 九   1   NU :   nine

gauh-nín 舊年   15   TW :   last year

ge 嘅   4   P :   indicating modification

géi 幾   7   ADV :   quite

gei-dāk 記得   13   V :   remember

géi(-dō) chín 幾(多)錢   6   QW :   cost how much

géi(-dō)-dím 幾(多)點   7   QW :   what time

géi(-dō) houh 幾(多)號   5/13   QW :   what number; what date

géi(-dō)-yuht 幾(多)月   13   QW :   which month

géi-noih 幾耐   15   QW :   how long (time)

géi-sìh 幾時   13   QW :   when

gin 見   16   V :   meet

go 個   4   M :   counting people and many
                                          other objects

gó-douh 嗰度   3   PW :   there

góng 講   15   V :   to speak

gūng-sī 公司 (M: gàan 間)   5   N :   company

Hèung-góng 香港	13	PW :	Hong Kong
hó-lohk 可樂	9	N :	coke
hohk 學	15	V :	learn
hòi-wúi 開會	13	VO :	to hold a meeting
hóu 好	6	ADV/ ADJ :	very fine; good
hóu noih móuh gin 好耐冇見	4		Haven't seen you for a long time
hóu síu 好少	13	ADV :	rarely, seldom
hóu-sihk 好食	12	ADJ :	delicious
hóu-tái 好睇	15	ADJ :	interesting; good looking
hóu-tìn 好天	13	ADJ :	fine weather
houh 號	13	TW :	day (of a month), number
houh-jí 毫子	6	N :	ten cents
hùhng-sīk 紅色	6	N :	red

J

jàn-haih 眞係	12	ADV :	really
jáu 走	16	V :	leave, run
jáu-dim 酒店 (M: gàan 間)	14	PW :	hotel
jáu-làuh 酒樓 (M: gàan 間)	12	PW :	Chinese restaurant
jauh 就	14	CON :	(in case if) ... then
jeui 最	13	P :	most
jì 知	13	V :	to know (a fact)
ji 至	13	CON :	until

jí 紙 (M: Jèung 張)   11   N :   paper

jì-hauh 之後   16   TW : afterwards; later on

jí-sĭk 紫色   6   N :   purple

jihk heui 直去   3   V :   go straight

Jìm-sà-jéui 尖沙咀   12   PW : Tsim Sha Tsui

jit 折   6   N :   discount

V + jó 咗   11   VS : indicating completion

jóu-chāan 早餐   7   N :   breakfast

jóu-sàhn 早晨   2   Good morning

jouh 做   7   V :   to do

Jùng-gwok choi 中國菜   16   N :   Chinese cuisine

jùng-tàuh 鐘頭 (M: go 個)   15   TW : hour

Jùng-wàahn 中環   12   PW : Central

Jùng-wàahn Gwóng-chèuhng 12 PW : Central Plaza
    中環廣場

jùng-yi 鍾意   10   V/AV : like

jyuh 住   12   V :   live

jyun 轉   3   V :   turn

jyun jó 轉左   3   VO : turn left

jyun yauh 轉右   3   VO : turn right

K

kāat-pín 卡片   4   N :   name card; business
                                          card

kàhm-máahn 琴晚   8   TW : last night

kàhm-yaht 琴日   12   TW : yesterday

káhn 近	14	ADJ :	close to
kéuih 佢	4	PN :	he; she; it
kéuih-deih 佢哋	4	PN :	they
kìng 傾	15	V :	to chat; to discuss

L

lā 啦	6	FP :	let's; place
la 喇	3/5	FP :	already; indicating changes
laaht 辣	16	ADJ :	hot and spicy
làih 嚟	7	V :	come
láih-baai-luhk 禮拜六	13	TW :	Saturday
láih-baai-ńgh 禮拜五	13	TW :	Friday
láih-baai-sàam 禮拜三	13	TW :	Wednesday
láih-baai-sei 禮拜四	13	TW :	Thursday
láih-baai-yaht 禮拜日	13	TW :	Sunday
láih-baai-yāt 禮拜一	13	TW :	Monday
láih-baai-yih 禮拜二	13	TW :	Tuesday
láu 樓	12	N :	floor
leng 靚	6	ADJ :	beautiful
léuih-hàhng 旅行	13	N :	travel; picnic; trip
līp 軨 (M: ga 架)	14	N :	lift
lohk yúh 落雨	13	VO :	rain
luhk 六	1	NU :	six
luhk-sīk 綠色	6	N :	green

M

maahn 萬	10	NU :	ten thousand
máaih 買	10	V :	buy
maaih 賣	12	V :	sell
màaih dāan 埋單	10	VO :	check the bill
màh-fàahn 麻煩	13	ADJ :	troublesome
mahn 問	13	V :	to ask a question
māan 蚊	6	N :	dollar
māt-yéh 乜嘢	6	QW :	what; what kind of
māt-yéh sīk 乜嘢色	6	QW :	what colour
mē 咩	15	FP :	mood of surprise; what
meih 未	16	P :	not yet
Méih-sàm Jáu-làuh 美心酒樓	12	PW :	Maxim's Restaurant
m̀h 唔	4	P :	not
m̀h-gán-yiu 唔緊要	2		never mind
m̀h-gòi 唔該	2		thank you; excuse me; please
m̀h-gòi dáng dáng 唔該等等	2		wait a moment
m̀h-gòi dáng jahn 唔該等陣	2		wait a moment
m̀h-hái-douh 唔喺度	5		not here
m̀h-hōu-yi-sì 唔好意思	2		sorry
m̀h-sái 唔駛	2/11		no need to
m̀h-syù-fuhk 唔舒服	13	ADJ :	uncomfortable; sick
mòhng 忙	8	ADJ :	busy
móuh 冇	6	V :	opposite of 'yáuh'

mòuh-gān 毛巾間   11   N :   towel
(M: tìuh 條)

múih-yaht 每日   12   TW : everyday

mùhn-háu 門口   12   N :   entrance; doorway

N

náaih 奶   9   N :   milk

náaih-chàh 奶茶   9   N :   milk tea

nám 諗   15   V :   think

néih 你   4   PN : you

néih-deih 你哋   4   PN : you (plural)

Néih dím a? 你點呀？   4   How are you?

Néih hóu 你好   4   Nice to meet you

ńgh 五   1   NU : five

ngáahn-fan 眼瞓   8   ADJ : sleepy

ngāam 啱   12   ADJ : correct

ngàh-chīm 牙籤   11   N :   toothpicks

ngàhn-hòhng 銀行   14   PW : bank
(M: gàan 間)

ngàhn-sīk 銀色   6   N :   silver

ngóh 我   4   PN : I; me

ngóh-deih 我哋   4   PN : we

Ngóh dōu haih 我都係   10   Me too

ni-douh 呢度   3   PW : here

nī-go yuht 呢個月   13   TW : this month

nìhn 年   15   TW : year

nìhng-mūng chàh 檸檬茶   9   N： lemon tea

nìng-jáu 擰走   9   V： take away; carry out

noih 耐   15   ADJ： very long time

P

pàhng-yáuh 朋友   4   N： friend

pèhng 平   6   ADJ： cheap

pìhng-sìh 平時   15   TW： usually

pou-táu 舖頭 (M: gàan 間)   14   PW： shop

S

sàam 三   1   NU： three

sāam 衫 (M: gihn 件)   12   N： clothes

sàang-yaht 生日   13   N： birthday

sahp 十   1   NU： ten

sai 細   6   ADJ： small

sái-sáu-gāan 洗手間   14   PW： toilet
(M: go 個)

Sàm-jan 深圳   15   PW： Shenzhen

sàn 新   6   ADJ： new

Sàn Sai-gaai Daaih-hah   14   PW： New World Tower
新世界大廈

sāp 濕   13   ADJ： wey; humid

sé-jih-làuh 寫字樓   12   PW： office
(M: go 個)

sei 四   1   NU： four

seuhng-go láih-baai 上個禮拜	13	TW :	last week
seuhng-go sìng-kèih 上個星期	13	TW :	last week
seuhng-go yuht 上個月	13	TW :	last month
seuhng-mihn 上面	14	PW :	above; on top of
seuhng-nín 上年	15	TW :	last year
séui 水	10	N :	water
séung 想	6/10	AV :	want to; wish to
sìh-sìh 時時	13	ADV :	very often; always
sihk 食	7	V :	eat
sihk aan 食晏	7	VO :	have lunch
sihk faahn 食飯	7	VO :	have a meal
sihk jóu-chāan 食早餐	7	VO :	have breakfast
sihk máahn-faahn 食晚飯	7	VO :	have dinner
sīk 識	14	V :	know how to; have knowledge of; to know (somebody)
sìn 先	16	A :	first
sìn-sàang 先生	4	N :	Mr; husband; teacher
sing 姓	4	V :	surname
sìng-kèih-luhk 星期六	13	TW :	Saturday
sìng-kèih-ńgh 星期五	13	TW :	Friday
sìng-kèih-sàam 星期三	13	TW :	Wednesday
sìng-kèih-sei 星期四	13	TW :	Thursday
sìng-kèih-yaht 星期日	13	TW :	Sunday

sìng-kèih-yāt 星期一	13	TW :	Monday
sìng-kèih-yih 星期二	13	TW :	Tuesday
síu 少	8	ADJ :	little; less
síu-bā 小巴 (M: ga 架)	3	N :	minibus
síu-jé 小姐	4	N :	Miss; young lady
síu-síu 少少	14	ADJ :	a little
syù 書 (M: bún 本)	11	N :	book
syù-dim 書店 (M: gàan 間)	12	PW :	book store
syù-fuhk 舒服	13	ADJ :	comfortable
syùhn 船 (M: jek 隻)	3	N :	ferry; boat
syùn 酸	16	ADJ :	sour

T

Taai-gwok choi 泰國菜	16	N :	Thai food
taai-táai 太太	4	N :	Mrs; wife; lady (married)
tái dihn-sih 睇電視	7	VO :	watch television
tái-háh 睇吓	6		take a look; depend on
tái hei 睇戲	16	VO :	see movie
tèng 聽	16	V :	listen; hear
tìhm 甜	16	ADJ :	sweet
tìhng 停	3	V :	stop
tìhng-chè-cheùhng 停車場 (M: go 個)	12	PW :	car park
tìn-hei 天氣	13	N :	weather
Tìn-sīng Máh-tàuh 天星碼頭	12	PW :	Star Ferry Pier

tìng-máahn 聽晚	16	TW :	tomorrow night
tìng-yaht 聽日	10	TW :	tomorrow
tòhng 糖	9	N :	sugar
tói 枱 (M: jèung 張)	11	N :	table
tòng 湯	11	N :	soup
tóuh-ngoh 肚餓	8	ADJ :	hungry
tùhng(-màaih) 同（埋）	8	CON :	and; together with
Tùhng-lòh-wāan 銅鑼灣	12	PW :	Causeway Bay
tùhng-sih 同事	4	N :	colleague

U

| ūk-kéi 屋企 | 5 | N : | home |

W

waahk-jé 或者	13	ADV :	may be
wáan 玩	13	V :	have fun; play
Wāan-jái 灣仔	13	PW :	Wanchai
wán 搵	5	V :	look for; search
wòhng-sīk 黃色	6	N :	yellow
wúih 會	15	AV :	will probably
wún 碗 (M: jek 隻 / go 個)	9	N :	bowl

Y

yàhn 人 (M: go 個)	11	N :	people
yaht 日	15	TW :	day
Yaht-bún choi 日本菜	16	N :	Japanese food

yám 飲	10	V :	drink
yám-bùi 飲杯	11	VO :	cheers!; have a drink
yàm-tìn 陰天	13	N :	cloudy
yàn-waih 因爲	8	CON :	because
yāt 一	1	NU :	one
yāt-chàih 一齊	8	A :	together
yāt-jahn 一陣	15	TW :	a moment, later
yáuh 有	6	V :	possess; have; exist
yáuh-sìh 有時	10/13	A :	sometimes
yeh-máahn 夜晚	12	TW :	night
Yi-daaih-leih choi 意大利菜	16	N :	Italian food
yih 二	1	NU :	two
yìh-gā 而家	8	TW :	now
yiht 熱	9	ADJ :	hot
yìn-fùi-gòng 煙灰缸 (M: go 個)	11	N :	ashtray
Yìng-màhn 英文	11	N :	English
Yìng-màhn syù 英文書	11	N :	English book
yiu 要	9	V/AV :	want; need
yú 魚 (M: tìuh 條)	11	N :	fish
yùh-gwó 如果	14	CON :	if
yuht 月	13	TW :	month
Yuht-nàahm choi 越南菜	16	N :	Vietnamese food

Appendix 2

English to Cantonese

A

above	seuhng-mihn 上面, seuhng-bihn 上便
Admiralty	Gām-jūng 金鐘
afterwards	jì-hauh 之後
always	sìh-sìh 時時
and	tùhng(-màaih) 同（埋）
approximately	N + dóu 倒
ashtray	yìn-fùi-gòng 煙灰缸 (M: go 個)
ask	mahn 問 (question)
at	hái 喺

B

back	hauh-mihn 後面, hauh-bihn 後便
bank	ngàhn-hòhng 銀行 (M: gàan 間)
BBQ pork bun	chà-sìu-bāau 叉燒包
BBQ pork with rice	chà-sìu faahn 叉燒飯
beautiful	leng 靚
because	yàn-waih 因為
beer	bē-jáu 啤酒

because	yàn-waih 因爲
beer	bē-jáu 啤酒
before	jì-chìhn 之前
below	hah-mihn 下面, hah-bihn 下便
big	daaih 大
bill	dāan 單 (M: jèung 張)
birthday	sàang-yaht 生日
bitter	fú 苦
black	hāk-sīk 黑色
blue	làahm-sīk 藍色
boat	syùhn 船 (M: jek 隻)
book	syù 書 (M: bún 本)
book store	syù-dim 書店 (M: gàan 間)
bowl	wún 碗 (M: jek 隻 / go 個)
(have) breakfast	sihk jóu-chāan 食早餐
brown	(ga-)fē-sīk（咖）啡色
bus	bā-sí 巴士 (M: ga 架)
business card	kāat-pín 卡片 (M: go 個 / jèung 張)
busy	mòhng 忙
but	daahn-haih 但係
buy	máaih 買

C

can	dāk 得
Cantonese	Gwóng-dùng-wá 廣東話

car park	tìhng-chè-chèuhng 停車場 (M: go 個)
Causeway Bay	Tùhng-lòh-wāan 銅鑼灣
Central	Jùng-wàahn 中環
chair	dang 凳 (M: jèung 張)
chat	kìng 傾
cheap	pèhng 平
cheers!	yám-bùi 飲杯
Chinese cuisine	Jùng-gwok choi 中國菜
Chinese language	Jùng-màhn 中文
chopsticks	faai-jí 筷子 (M: deui 對 / sèung 雙)
close to	káhn 近
clothes	sāam 衫 (M: gihn 件)
cloudy	yàm-tìn 陰天
coat	lāu 褸 (M: gihn 件)
coca cola	hó-lohk 可樂
coffee	ga-fē 咖啡
cold	dung 凍
colleague	tùhng-sih 同事
come	làih 嚟
comfortable	syù-fuhk 舒服
company	gūng-sī 公司 (M: gàan 間)
convenient	fòng-bihn 方便
correct	ngāam 啱
cost how much	géi(-dō) chín 幾 (多) 錢
cup	būi 杯 (M: jek 隻 / go 個)

D

date	houh 號
day	yaht 日
degree	douh 度
delicious	hóu-sihk 好食
dim sum	dím-sām 點心
(have) dinner	sihk máahn-faahn 食晚飯
discount	jit 折
discuss	kìng 傾
do	jouh 做
dollar	mān 蚊
drink	yám 飲

E

eat	sihk 食 / sihk-faahn 食飯
eat here	hái douh sihk 喺度食
eight	baat 八
English	Yìng-màhn 英文
enjoy	wáan 玩
entrance	mùhn-háu 門口 (M: go 個)
everyday	múih-yaht 每日
excuse me	m̀h-gòi 唔該; m̀h-hóu-yi-sì 唔好意思
expensive	gwai 貴

F

fast	faai 快

ferry	syùhn 船 (M: jek 隻)
fine weather	hóu-tìn 好天
first	sìn 先
fish	yú 魚 (M: tìuh 條)
five	ńgh or ḿh 五
floor	láu 樓
forget	m̀h-gei-dāk 唔記得
four	sei 四
free (time)	dāk-hàahn 得閒
Friday	láih-baai-ńgh 禮拜五 / sìng-kèih-ńgh 星期五
friend	pàhng-yáuh 朋友
front	chìhn-mihn 前面 / chìhn-bihn 前便
full (stomach)	báau 飽

G

give	béi 畀
glass	būi 杯 (M: jek 隻 /go 個)
go	heui 去
go home	fàan ūk-kéi 返屋企
go straight	jihk heui 直去
gold (colour)	gām-sīk 金色
good	hóu 好
Good morning	jóu-sàhn 早晨
goodbye	bāai-baai 拜拜
green	luhk-sīk 綠色

grey	fùi-sīk 灰色
ground	deih-há 地下

H

have	yáuh 有
haven't	móuh 冇
Haven't seen you for a long time	Hóu noih móuh gin 好耐冇見
he	kéuih 佢
hear	tèng 聽
here	nī-douh 呢度
(have a) holiday	fong-ga 放假
home	ūk-kéi 屋企
Hong Kong	Hèung-góng 香港
hot	yiht 熱
hotel	jáu-dim 酒店 (M: gàan 間)
hour	jùng-tàuh 鐘頭
How are you?	Néih dím a? 你點呀？
how long (time)	géi-noih or géi-loih 幾耐
how many	géi-dō 幾多
hundred	baak 百
hungry	tóuh-ngoh 肚餓

I

I	ngóh 我
if	yùh-gwó 如果

in	hái 喺
interesting	hóu-tái 好睇 (see or read); hóu-wáan 好玩 (have fun)
invite	chéng 請
invoice	dāan 單 (M: jèung 張)
Italian food	Yi-daaih-leih choi 意大利菜

J

Japanese food	Yaht-bún choi 日本菜

K

know	jì 知 (facts); sīk 識 (knowledge; people)

L

large	daaih 大
last month	seuhng-go yuht 上個月
last night	kàhm-máahn 琴晚
last week	seuhng-go láih-baai 上個禮拜 / seuhng-go sìng-kèih 上個星期
last year	gauh-nín 舊年 / seuhng-nín 上年
late	chìh-dou 遲到 / chìh 遲
later	chìh-dī 遲啲
later on	jì-hauh 之後
learn	hohk 學
leave	jáu 走

lemon tea	nìhng-mūng-chàh or lìhng-mūng-chàh 檸檬茶
Let me introduce	Dáng ngóh làih gaai-siuh 等我嚟介紹
lift	līp 較 (M: go 個 / ga 架)
like	jùng-yi 鍾意
listen	tèng 聽
live	jyuh 住
look for	wán 搵
lunch	sihk-aan 食晏

M

market	gàai-síh 街市 (M: go 個)
Maxim's Restaurant	Méih-sām Jáu-làuh 美心酒樓
may be	waahk-jé 或者
may I ask?	chéng-mahn 請問
meet	gin 見
meeting	hòi-wúi 開會
milk	náaih 奶
milk tea	náaih-chàh 奶茶
minibus	síu-bā 小巴
minute	fàn-jùng 分鐘 (time spent); fàn 分
Miss	síu-jé 小姐
Misses	taai-táai 太太
Mister	sìn-sàang 先生
Monday	láih-baai-yāt 禮拜一 / sìng-kèih-yāt 星期一
month	yuht 月

more	dò-dī 多啲; ADJ + dī 啲
more than	ADJ + gwo 過
most	jeui 最
movie	hei 戲; tái hei 睇戲 (see movie)
MTR	deih-tit 地鐵
MTR station	deih-tit-jaahm 地鐵站 (M: go 個)

N

nearby	fuh-gahn 附近
never mind	m̀h-gán-yiu 唔緊要
new	sàn 新
newspaper	bou-jí 報紙 (M: fahn 份)
next month	hah-go yuht 下個月
next week	hah-go láih-baai 下個禮拜 / hah-go sìng-kèi 下個星期個
next year	chēut-nín 出年 / hah-nín 下年
Nice to meet you	Néih hóu 你好
night	yeh-máahn 夜晚
nine	gáu 九
no need to	m̀h-sái 唔駛
not here	m̀h-hái-douh 唔喺度
not yet	meih 未
now	yìh-gā 而家

O

o'clock	dím 點

O.K.	dāk 得
office	sé-jih-làuh 寫字樓 (M: go 個)
one	yāt 一
oneself	jih-géi 自己
opposite side	deui-mihn 對面
or	dihng(-haih) 定 (係)
orange (colour)	cháang-sīk 橙色

P

paper	jí 紙 (M: jèung 張)
pen	bāt 筆 (M: jì 枝)
people	yàhn 人 (M: go 個)
pink	fán-hùhng-sīk 粉紅色
please	m̀h-gòi 唔該
plenty	hóu dò 好多
poor	séui pèih 水皮 (poor skill)
	móuh chín 冇錢 (no money)
purple	jí-sīk 紫色

Q

quick	faai 快; faai-dī 快啲 (quickly, faster)
quite	géi 幾個

R

rain	lohk yúh 落雨
rarely	hóu síu 好少

really	jàn-haih 眞係
receipt	dāan 單 (M: jèung 張)
recently	jeui-gahn 最近
red	hùhng-sīk 紅色
remember	gei-dāk 記得
reserve table	dehng tói 訂枱 (table)
restaurant	chāan-tēng 餐廳 (M: gàan 間)
	jáu-làuh 酒樓 (chinese restaurant)
rice	faahn 飯

S

salty	hàahm 鹹
Saturday	làih-baai-luhk 禮拜六 /
	sìng-kèih-luhk 星期六
sell	maaih 賣
seven	chāt 七
she	kéuih 佢
shoes	hàaih 鞋 (M: deui 對)
shop	pou-táu 舖頭 (M: gàan 間)
sick	m̀h-syù-fuhk 唔舒服
silver (colour)	ngàhn-sīk 銀色
six	luhk 六
sleep	fan-gaau 瞓覺
sleepy	ngáahn-fan 眼瞓
small	sai 細
sometimes	yáuh-sìh 有時

sorry	m̀h-hóu-yi-sì 唔好意思 / deui-m̀h-jyuh 對唔住
soup	tòng 湯
sour	syùn 酸
speak	góng 講
spicy	laaht 辣
spoon	chìh-gāng 匙羹 (M: jek 隻)
stop	tìhng 停
street conrner	gàai-háu 街口 (M: go 個)
sugar	tòhng 糖
Sunday	láih-baai-yaht 禮拜日 / sìng-kèih-yaht 星期日
sweet	tìhm 甜

T

table	tói 枱 (M: jèung 張)
take a transport	daap-chè 搭車
takeaway	nìng-jáu or lìng-jáu 擰走
taxi	dīk-sí 的士 (M: ga 架)
telephone	dihn-wá 電話 (M: go 個); dá dihn-wá 打電話 (make a phone call)
ten	sahp 十
ten thousand	maahn 萬
Thai food	Taai-gwok choi 泰國菜
thank you	m̀h-gòi 唔該; dò-jeh 多謝 (for gifts or meals, congratulations, invitations, appreciation)

that	gó 嗰 + M
That's all	Haih gam dò la 係咁多喇
then	jauh 就; jì-hauh 之後
there	gó-douh 嗰度
they	kéuih-deih 佢哋
thing	yéh 嘢
thirsty	háu-hot 口渴
this month	nì-go yuht 呢個月 / gàm-go yuht 今個月
this week	gàm-go láih-baai 今個禮拜 / gàm-go sìng-kèih 今個星期
this year	gàm-nín or gàm-nìhn 今年
thousand	chìn 千
three	sàam 三
Thursday	láih-baai-sei 禮拜四 / sìng-kèih-sei 星期四
times	chi 次
tired	gwuih 劫
today	gàm-yaht 今日
toilet	sái-sáu-gāan 洗手間 (M: go 個)
tomorrow	tìng-yaht 聽日
tomorrow night	tìng-máahn 聽晚
traffic light	dāng-wái 燈位
travel	léuih-hàhng 旅行 (M: chi 次)
troublesome	màh-fàahn 麻煩
Tsim Sha Tsui	Jìm-sà-jéui 尖沙咀
Tuesday	láih-baai-yih 禮拜二 / sìng-kèih-yih 星期二
turn left	jyun jó 轉左

turn right	jyun yauh 轉右
two	yih 二; léuhng 兩 + M

U

until	ji 至
usually	pìhng-sìh 平時

V

vegetables	choi 菜
Vietnamese food	Yuht-nàahm choi 越南菜
visit	wàn 搵

W

wait a moment	m̀h-gòi dáng dáng 唔該等等 / m̀h-gòi dáng jahn 唔該等陣
walk	hàahng-louh 行路
Wan Chai	Wāan-jái 灣仔
want	yiu 要 / séung yiu 想要
want to	séung 想
watch TV	tái dihn-sih 睇電視
water	séui 水
we	ngóh-deih 我哋
weather	tìn-hei 天氣
Wednesday	láih-baai-sāam 禮拜三 / sìng-kèih-sāam 星期三
well	gám 咁

wet	sāp 濕
what	māt-yéh 乜嘢; mē 咩
what colour	māt-yéh sīk 乜嘢色
what's your surname?	gwai sing a? 貴姓呀?
what time	géi(-dō)-dím 幾（多）點
when	géi-sìh 幾時
where	bīn-douh 邊度
which month	bīn-go yuht 邊個月 / géi(-dō)-yuht 幾（多）月
white	baahk-sīk 白色
who	bīn-go 邊個
why	dím-gáai 點解
will	wúih 會
work	fàan-gùng 返工 (go to work); jouh-yéh 做嘢
wrong number	dá-cho 打錯

Y

year	nìhn 年
yellow	wòhng-sīk 黃色
yesterday	kàhm-yaht 琴日
you	néih 你; néih-deih 你哋 (plural)

Appendix 3

Cantonese to Putonghua

Cantonese	Lesson	Putonghua
Cantonese	*Lesson*	*Putonghua*

B

bāsí 巴士	3	gōnggòng qìchē 公共汽车
béi 畀	12	gěi 给
bīn-douh 邊度	13	nǎli 哪里, nǎr 哪儿
bīn-go 邊個	4	shuí, shéi 谁
bīn-go yuht 邊個月	14	nǎge yuè, něige yuè 哪个月

C

| chēut-nín 出年 | 16 | míngnián 明年 |
| chìh-dī dá-làih 遲啲打嚟 | 5 | guò yíhuìr dálái 过一会儿打来 |

D

dá cho 打錯	5	bō cuò le 拨错了
daap līp 搭粒	15	zuò diàntī 坐电梯; zuò shēngjiàngjī 坐升降机
dāk 得	6	kěyǐ 可以
dāk-hàahn 得閒	8	yǒukòng 有空

dang 凳	12	yǐzi 椅子	
Dáng ngóh làih gaai-siuh 等我嚟介紹	4	Ràng wǒ lái jièshaò 让我来介绍	
dāngwái 燈位	3	jiāotōng dēng 交通灯	
dehng tói 訂枱	12	dìng zhuō 订桌	
dī 啲	4	yìdiǎnr 一点儿; yìxiē 一些	
dihng(-haih) 定(係)	10	háishi 还是	
dīksí 的士	3	chūzū chē 出租车	
dím-gáai 點解	7	wèishénme 为什么	
dóu 倒	16	dàgài 大概	
dung 凍	10	lěng 冷	

F

fàan-gùng 返工	7	shàngbān 上班	
fàan ūk-kéi 返屋企	7	huíjiā 回家	
fan-gaau 瞓覺	7	shuìjiào 睡觉	

G

gàai-háu 街口	3	lùkǒu 路口	
gàai-síh 街市	15	cài shìchǎng 菜市场	
gám 噉	13	nàme 那么	
gàm-go láih-baai 今個禮拜	14	zhèige xīngqī 这个星期	
gàm-go yuht 今個月	14	zhèige yuè 这个月	
gàm-yaht 今日	11	jīntiān 今天	
gauh-nín 舊年	16	qùnián 去年	
ge 嘅	4	de 的	

géi 幾 | 7 | tǐng 挺, xiāngdāng 相当
géi(-dō) chín 幾（多）錢 | 6 | duōshao qián 多少钱
géi(-dō) dím 幾（多）點 | 7 | jǐ diǎn 几点
géi(-dō) houh 幾（多）號 | 5 | jǐ hào 几号
géi(-dō) yuht 幾（多）月 | 14 | jǐ yuè 几月
géi-noih 幾耐 | 16 | duō jiǔ 多久
géi-sìh 幾時 | 14 | shéme shíhou 什么时候
gó-douh 嗰度 | 13 | nàli 那裏, nàr 那儿
gwán-séui 滾水 | 11 | rè kāishuǐ 热开水
gwuih 劫 | 7 | lèi 累

H

hàahng-louh 行路 | 3 | zǒu lù 走路
hái 喺 | 13 | zài 在
hái-douh sihk 喺度食 | 10 | zài zhèr chī 在这儿吃
haih 係 | 4 | shì 是
haih gam dò la 係咁多啦 | 12 | wán le 完了
hóu 好 (ADV) | 6 | hěn 很
hóu noih móuh gin 好耐冇見 | 4 | hěn jiǔ méi jiàn 很久没见
hóu-sihk 好食 | 13 | hǎo chī 好吃
hóu-síu 好少 | 14 | hěn shǎo 很少
hóu-tái 好睇 | 17 | hǎo kàn 好看
hóu-tìn 好天 | 14 | tiānqíng 天晴
hòuh-jí 毫子 | 6 | máo 毛

J

jàn-haih 眞係	12	zhēn 真; zhēn shi 真是
jáu 走	15	líkāi 离开
jihk heui 直去	3	yìzhí zǒu 一直走
jóu-sàhn 早晨	2	zǎo shàng hǎo 早上好
jùng-yi 鍾意	11	xǐhuan 喜欢

K

kāat-pín 卡片	4	míngpiàn 名片
kàhm-máahn 琴晚	8	zuótiān wǎnshang 昨天晚上
kàhm-yaht 琴日	12	zuótiān 昨天
kéuih 佢	4	tā 他 / 她 / 它
kéuih-deih 佢哋	4	tāmen 他们
kìng 傾	16	tán 谈

L

lā 啦	6	ba 吧
la 喇	5	le 了
leng 靚	6	měi 美 / piāoliang 漂亮
lèuhng 涼	12	liǎngkuài 凉快
līp 粒	15	diàntī 电梯
lohk-yúh 落雨	14	xiàyǔ 下雨

M

m̀h 唔	4	bù 不

nī 呢 + M	4	zhè 这
nī-douh 呢度	3	zhèli 这里, zhèr 这儿
nī-go yuht 呢個月	14	zhèige yuè 这个月
nìng-jáu 擰走	9	qúzǒu 取走
noih 耐	16	jiǔ 久

P

pèhng 平	6	piányi 便宜
pìhng-sìh 平時	13	yìbān 一般, píngcháng 平常
pou-táu 舖頭	15	shàngdiàn 商店

S

sāam 衫	13	yīfu 衣服
sai 細	6	xiǎo 小
sé-jih-làuh 寫字樓	13	bàngōnglóu 办公楼
sìh-sìh 時時	14	chángcháng 常常
sihk 食	7	chī 吃
sihk-faahn 食飯	7	chīfàn 吃饭
sīk 識	15	dǒng 懂, rènshi 认识
sìn-sàang 先生	4	xiānshang 先生, zhàngfu 丈夫

T

tái dihn-sih 睇電視	7	kàn diànshì 看电视
tái-háh 睇吓	6	kàn-yíxià 看一下
tái-hei 睇戲	17	kàn diànyǐng 看电影

Appendix 4
Some Cantonese Slang

(CD 3, Track 35)

a-jē 阿姐	a very competent lady
AA jai ＡＡ制	share the bill, go Dutch
àau-saai tàuh 撓晒頭	completely lost (in an idea) (lit: scratch one's head)
baahn-yéh 扮嘢	pretend to be important
báai wù-lúng 擺烏龍	make a mistake
baat-gwa 八卦	nosy
bāau-mēi or bāau-méih 包尾	at the end of the list
baih lak 弊嘞	That's too bad
béi-háh mín 畀吓面	give me some face
bok-mehng 搏命	work desperately
bok-yāt-bok 搏一搏	try one's luck
bun-túng-séui 半桶水	having only a little knowledge (lit: half bucket of water)

(CD 3, Track 36)

chaat-hàaih-jái 擦鞋仔	a 'yes' man (lit: shoe-shine boy)
cháau gwu-piu 炒股票	to speculate on stocks and shares
cháau láu 炒樓	to speculate on real estate properties

cháau yàuh-yú 炒魷魚	to dismiss someone (from his job) (lit: stir-fry squid)
chèuhng-hei 長氣	long-winded
chéun-gwo jek jyù 蠢過隻豬	more stupid than a pig
chēut-wái 出位	doing what one should not do; outstanding
chì-sin 黐線	crazy (lit: wires crossed)
chói néih dōu sòh 睬你都傻	It won't bother about you
chòu-lóuh 粗魯	rude

(CD 3, Track 37)

dá-dāk síu 打得少	deserve beating up
dá-gēi 打機	to play computer games
dá-jìm 打尖	to jump queue
dá ngàh-gaau 打牙較	to chat
dá syù-sou 打輸數	prepare for the worst
dá-wàahng-làih góng 打橫嚟講	being unreasonable
daaih-bá 大把	have a lot of; in abundance
daaih-lóu 大佬	big brother; a leader of a gang
daaih-múng 大懵	stupid
daaih-saai 大晒	appearing to be the most authoritative
daaih-tàuh-hā 大頭蝦	absent-minded (lit: a big headed prawn)
daaih-yi 大意	careless
daaih-yíh-lūng 大耳窿	a loanshark (lit: big ear hole)
daap-tói 搭枱	to share a table

dái-séi 抵死	ask for it
dái-sek 抵錫	deserving favour
dāk-daahm-siu 得啖笑	the gain is only marginal (lit: just for a laugh)
dāk ga la 得㗎喇	That's OK.; That's good enough
dāk-jó 得咗	having made it
dám sàm-háu 揼心口	to regret; pound one's chest
dihng-dī làih 定啲嚟	keep calm; be calm
dím-syun hóu 點算好？	what can be done?
díng-m̀h-seuhn 頂唔順	cannot put up with
dohng-sāt louh 蕩失路	get lost on the way
dūk bui-jek 篤背脊	backstab
dyun-gú 斷估	pure guesswork

(CD 3, Track 38)

fáan-mín 反面	become enemies, suddenly turn hostile
faat-daaht 發達	lucky, make a fortune
faat ngauh-dauh 發吽豆	look dull or bored
faat pèih-hei 發脾氣	lose one's temper
fong fèi-gèi 放飛機	stood somebody up
fong gwo ngóh 放過我	leave me alone; give me a break
fut-lóu 濶佬	generous
gáau bīn-fō a? 搞邊科呀？	What are you trying to do?
gáau cho a! 搞錯呀！	It's a mistake!
gáau-dihm 搞掂	It's done!
gáau-gáau-jan 搞搞震	goofing around
gáau-siu 搞笑	hilarious

gáu-m̀h-daap-baat 九唔搭八   be unrelated

gihng 勁   powerful

gīk-hei 激氣   irritated; annoyed

gīk-séi-yàhn 激死人   very irritating; very annoying

gwàan léih mē sih 關你咩事   none of your business

gwai dou fèi-héi 貴到飛起   outrageously expensive

gwo-dāk-heui 過得去   passable

gwú-waahk 古惑   cunning, street smart

(CD 3, Track 39)

hāak(-jái) 黑（仔）   have bad luck

hāan chín 慳錢   save money

haih-gám-yí 係咁意   just a bit

háu-sò 口疏   not able to keep secrets

hèung(-jó) 香（咗）   to be dead; It's a failure

hóu gwo móuh 好過冇   better than nothing

ja-dai 咋帝   to pretend

jà-fīt 揸弗   be in charge

jai-m̀h-gwo 制唔過   not worth it

jāp-lāp 執笠   to close down (a shop or company)

jáu-bóu 走寶   miss a good chance

jáu-gāi 走雞   miss a chance (lit: run away a chicken)

jeng 正   excellent

jeuhk-sou 着數   advantagous

jihng-gāi-gāi 靜雞雞   very quietly; sneakily

jíng-dihng 整定	pre-destined
jíng-gwú 整蠱	to play a trick on someone
jok daaih 作大	embellish; boast; exaggerate
jyù-pàhng-gáu-yáuh 豬朋狗友	friends with bad habits (lit: pig friends dog pals)
jyù-tàuh-bíng 豬頭丙	fool; blockhead

(CD 3, Track 40)

kùhng-gwái 窮鬼	a very poor person
lá-yìhng 乸型	a very effferminate man
làahm-yàhn-pòh 男人婆	a tomboy
laahp-saap 垃圾	rubbish; trash
lahp-láp-lyuhn 立立亂	in disorder
lauh-hei 漏氣	slow in action or decision making
léih góng yéh àh? 你講嘢吖？	Are you talking nonsense?
lèih-póu 離譜	illogical; unreasonable
léih wah sih 你話事	You make the decision; It's all up to you
lēng-jái 靚仔	young boy
lēng-mūi 靚妹	young girl
leuhn-jeuhn 論盡	clumsy
lēuk-séui 掠水	to squeeze money from people; to tap water
lóuh-béng 老餅	old fashioned
lóuh-dím 老點	make a fool of somebody
lóuh-fúng 老奉	take things for granted
lóuh-tóu 老土	old-fashioned
lyún-làih 亂嚟	do things irresponsibly

(CD 3, Track 41)

máih chòuh 咪嘈	shut up
m̀h-chì-gà 唔黐家	never at home
m̀h-deui-louh 唔對路	it doesn't look right
m̀h-gok-yi 唔覺意	unintentionally
m̀h-gwàan léih sih 唔關你事	none of your business
m̀h-jì góng māt 唔知講乜	don't know what to say/don't know what he's talking about
m̀h-sái jí-yi 唔使指意	don't count on (someone)
m̀h-sái séi 唔使死	it doesn't cost your life
móuh fùh 冇符	no way out
móuh gam hóu hei 冇咁好氣	would not give any attention to it
móuh léih fán 冇你份	you are not included
mòuh-lèih-tàuh 無厘頭	expressions or actions that mean nothing
móuh líu 冇料	not knowledgeable
móuh mín 冇面	lose face
móuh ngáahn tái 冇眼睇	hate to see it
móuh nóuh 冇腦	brainless
móuh sàm-gèi 冇心機	feeling melancholy
móuh yáhn 冇癮	weary; lack of interest
móuh yi-gin 冇意見	no comment
mùhng-chàh-chàh 矇查查	in a muddle vision
ngāam-kì 啱 key	to get along well (with people) (lit: the right key or tone in music)

ngohng-gèui 戇居	indifferent to hints, stupid

(CD 3, Track 42)

sàai hei 嘥氣	waste of effort
sài-leih 犀利	extreme
sàm-jiu 心照	understand without the need for words
sàm-lèuhng 心涼	feel avenged
sàm-táahm 心淡	losing hope
sāp-sāp-seui 濕濕碎	miscellaneous; trivial
sāt-wàhn-yú 失魂魚	an absent-minded person
sàu sèng 收聲	shut up
sèh-wòhng 蛇王	to sneak away
sek-saai léih 錫晒你	you're my favourite, I love you so much
sèui dou séi 衰到死	you're so bad
séui-fo 水貨	imported goods without an agent ('parallel' imports)
sèui-jó 衰咗	to have failed
sih-daahn 是但	do as you like; whatever
sihk gūk-júng 食穀種	living on one's savings
sihk séi-māau 食死貓	falsely accused (lit: eat a dead cat)
siht-dái 蝕底	to lose out
sīk jouh 識做	know what is the smart thing to do
sīk taan 識嘆	know how to enjoy life
síng-muhk 醒目	smart
síu-hei 小器	narrow-minded
sìu-yé 宵夜	midnight snack
sòh gàh néih? 傻㗎你？	Are you crazy?; Are you nuts?

sòh-lóu 傻佬	a fool; an idot

(CD 3, Track 43)

tàhn-gāi 騰雞	timid and not decisive (lit: nervous chicken)
tái-síu 睇小	to belittle someone
tūng-déng 通頂	working overnight
wáan-yéh 玩嘢	provoke people
wáan-yùhn 玩完	game over
wah jì léih 話之你	not care what happens; who cares!
waht-daht 核突	disgusting, ugly
waih-sihk māau 爲食貓	greedy; glutton
wán-bahn 搵笨	looking for a sucker
wū-jōu 污糟	dirty
yài yài 曳曳	naughty (child)
yàm-sāp 陰濕	treacherous
yāt-chi-gwo 一次過	all in one go
yāt-sìh yāt-yeuhng 一時一樣	always changing (lit: one time one appearance)
yáuh líu 有料	knowledgeable
yáuh móuh gáau cho a? 有冇搞錯呀？	Have you made a mistake?; Are you for real?
yáuh-yìhng 有型	smart looking; cool
yéung-sèui 樣衰	bad looking (makes people dislike it)
yú dou bei 瘀到痺	very embarassing (lit: bruised to paralyzed)
yuhk-tung 肉痛	feel hurt when one lets something go (lit: the flesh is aching)

Suggested Answers

LESSON 2

Review Exercise — What do you say?

1. M̀h-gòi. 唔該。
2. jóu-sàhn. 早晨。
3. M̀h-sái 唔駛。
4. M̀h-gòi. 唔該。
5. M̀h-hóu yi-sì. Ngóh chìh-dou. 唔好意思。我遲到。
6. M̀h-gòi dáng dáng. 唔該等等。
7. M̀h-gán-yiu. 唔緊要。
8. M̀h-gòi. 唔該。
9. Dò-jeh. 多謝。
10. Bāai-baai. 拜拜。
11. M̀h-hóu yi-sì. 唔好意思。
12. Bāai-baai. 拜拜。

LESSON 4

Practice

1. *a*   2. *b*   3. *c*   4. *b*   5. *a*   6. *a*   7. *c*   8. *a*

Review Exercise

I.   Fill in the blanks

1. haih 係
2. tùhng-sih 同事 / pàhng-yáuh 朋友
3. m̀h 唔
4. haih m̀h-haih...a 係唔係…呀
5. your name

II. Translation

1. Kéuih-deih haih m̀h-haih Hòh sìn-sàang ge tùhng-sih a?

   佢 哋 係 唔 係 何 先 生 嘅 同 事 呀 ?

2. Kéuih haih m̀h-haih néih taai-táai a?

   佢 係 唔 係 你 太 太 呀 ?

3. Chàhn síu-jé m̀h-haih Wòhng taai-táai ge pàhng-yáuh.

   陳 小 姐 唔 係 黃 太 太 嘅 朋 友 。

4. Kéuih haih kéuih-deih ge pàhng-yáuh, m̀h-haih ngóh tùhng-sih.

   佢 係 佢 哋 嘅 朋 友 ， 唔 係 我 同 事 。

Listening Exercise

I.

1. *d*   2. *d*   3. *a*   4. *c*

II.

1. *F*   2. *F*   3. *T*   4. *T*   5. *T*   6. *F*   7. *T*

LESSON 5

Review Exercise — Translation

1. Ngóh gūng-sī dihn-wá haih yih sàam gáu chāt lìhng sei yih baat.

   我 公 司 電 話 係 二 三 九 七 零 四 二 八 。

2. Kéuih dá dihn-wá béi Chàhn taai-táai.

   佢 打 電 話 畀 陳 太 太 。

3. Néih ūk-kéi dihn-wá haih m̀h-haih sàam luhk yih chāt ńgh luhk lìhng lìhng a?

你 屋 企 電 話 係 唔 係 三 六 二 七 五 六
零 零 呀 ?

4. Bīn-go dá dihn-wá béi ngóh a?

邊 個 打 電 話 畀 我 呀 ?

5. M̀h-hóu yi-sī, chéng néih chìh-dì dá-làih lā..

唔 好 意 思 ， 請 你 啲 遲 打 嚟 啦 。

Listening Exercise

1. *a*   2. *d*   3. *b*   4. *a*   5. *c*   6. *c*   7. *c*

LESSON 6

A. Money — Practice

II.

1. $18.4   2. $0.6   3. $63.5   4. $21.9   5. $57.2

6. $4.1   7. $35.3   8. $0.2   9. $89.4   10. $92.6

Review Exercise — Translation

1. yáuh móuh làahm-sīk ga?
   有 冇 藍 色 㗎 ?

2. pèhng-dī lā. Ńgh sahp-mān dāk lā.
   平 啲 啦 。 五 十 蚊 得 啦 。

3. Nī-go móuh cháang-sīk.
   呢 個 冇 橙 色 。

4. Māt-yéh sīk a?

    乜 嘢 色 呀 ？

5. Wòhng-sīk ge chāt-sahp ńgh mān, hùhng-sīk ge sàam-sahp
    baat mān.

    黃 色 嘅 七 十 五 蚊 ， 紅 色 嘅 三 十 八 蚊 。

6. Fán-hùhng-sīk ge yáuh móuh daaih-dī ga?

    粉 紅 色 嘅 有 冇 大 啲 㗎 ？

7. Bīn-go sàn-dī a?

    邊 個 新 啲 呀 ？

Listening Exercise

I.

1. *N*   2. *Y*   3. *Y*   4. *N*   5. *N*   6. *N*

II.

1. *c*   2. *d*   3. *b*   4. *a*   5. *b*   6. *c*

LESSON 7

Review Exercise — Translation

1. Néih géi-dím fàan ūk-kéi a?

    你 幾 點 返 屋 企 呀 ？

2. Ngóh yāt-dím sihk-aan.

    我 一 點 食 晏 。

3. Néih tùhng-sih sàam-dím-bun jouh māt-yéh a?

    你 同 事 三 點 半 做 乜 嘢 呀 ？

4.   Néih pàhng-yáuh géi-dím sihk jóu-chāan a?
     你　朋　友　幾　點　食　早　餐　呀？

5.   Kéuih sahp-yāt-dím-gáu fan-gaau.
     佢　十　一　點　九　瞓　覺　。

Listening Exercises

1. haih 係   2. 8:00   3. m̀h-haih 唔係   4. 6:30

5. 7:30   6. 11:00   7. daap 搭   8. m̀h-daap 唔搭

LESSON 8

Review Final Particles

1. la 喇, lā 啦   2. àh 吖   3. lā 啦   4. a 呀 or ga 㗎

5. a 呀   6. la 喇   7. lā 啦   8. ga 㗎

Review Exercise

I.   Rewrite sentences

1.   Ngóh ńgh-dím daap dīk-sí fàan ūk-kéi.
     我　五　點　搭　的　士　返　屋　企　。

2.   Kéuih-deih yāt-dím sihk-faahn.
     佢　哋　一　點　食　飯　。

3.   Kéuih m̀h-tùhng taai-táai sihk-faahn.
     佢　唔　同　太　太　食　飯　。

4.   Ngóh pàhng-yáuh hóu dāk-hàahn.
     我　朋　友　好　得　閒　。

II. Fill in the blanks

1. fàan-gùng 返工   4. m̀h-tùhng 唔同

2. sihk aan 食晏   5. tùhng 同, sihk-faahn 食飯

3. pàhng-yáuh 朋友

III. Translation

1. Ngóh baat-dím-bun fàan-gùng.

我 八 點 半 搭 巴 士 返 工 。

2. Kéuih-deih chāt-dím-sàam làih, (yìhn-hauh) sahp-dím-
bun fàan ūk-kéi.

佢 哋 七 點 三 來 ,（然 後） 十 點 半 返
屋 企 。

3. Ngóh m̀h-tùhng taai-táai sihk aan.

我 唔 同 太 太 食 晏 。

4. Ngóh m̀h-mòhng.

我 唔 忙 。

5. Kéuih hóu ngáahn-fan.

佢 好 眼 瞓 。

6. Néih tùhng bīn-go sihk-faahn a?

你 同 邊 個 食 飯 呀 ？

7. Ngóh yìh-gā fàan ūk-kéi.

我 而 家 返 屋 企 。

8. Ngóh tùhng pàhng-yáuh tái dihn-sih.

我 同 朋 友 睇 電 視 。

Listening Exercise

I. Multiple choice

    1. *d*   2. *d*   3. *a*   4. *b*

II.

    1. *a*   2. *a*   3. *a*   4. *a*   5. *a*   6. *d*

III.

    1. 7:10   2. 11:15   3. tùhng-sih 同事

    4. m̀h-haih 唔係   5. haih 係   6. m̀h-haih 唔係

LESSON 9

Practice

I.

    1. daaih hó-lohk 大可樂   5. dung ga-fē 凍咖啡

    2. yiht ga-fē 熱咖啡   6. dung nìhng-mùng-chàh
                                        凍檸檬茶
    3. dung náaih-chàh 凍奶茶

    4. yiht nìhng-mùng-chàh
        熱檸檬茶

LESSON 10

Review Exercise

I. Fill in the blanks

    1. yám 飲   2. m̀h-séung 唔想

3. m̀h-yám 唔飲   4. māt-yéh 乜嘢

5. jùng m̀h-jùng-yi sihk 鍾唔鍾意食

6. dihn-wá 電話 (or any object)

II. Rewrite sentences

1. Kéuih pàhng-yáuh séung máaih chè
   佢 朋 友 想 買 車 。

2. Néih yám m̀h-yám ga-fē a?
   你 飲 唔 飲 咖 啡 呀 ?

3. Chàhn sìn-sàang m̀h-jùng-yi fàan-gùng.
   陳 先 生 唔 鍾 意 返 工 。

4. Néih séung tùhng bīn-go sihk-faahn a?
   你 想 同 邊 個 食 飯 呀 ?

5. Néih yìh-gā jùng-yi jouh māt-yéh a?
   你 而 家 想 做 乜 嘢 呀 ?

III. Translation

1. Néih séung yiu māt-yéh a?
   你 想 要 乜 嘢 呀 ?

2. Mh-gòi béi sei-wún faahn ngóh.
   唔 該 畀 四 碗 飯 我 。

3. Ngóh m̀h-jùng-yi chìh-dou.
   我 唔 鍾 意 遲 到 。

4. Ngóh séung yiu yāt-bùi séui.
   我 想 要 一 杯 水 。

5. Kéuih séung màaih dihn-sin.

　佢　想　買　電　視　。

6. Néih tìng-yaht heui m̀h-heui yám-chàh a?

　你　聽　日　去　唔　去　飲　茶　呀？

7. Néih séung heui bīn-douh a?

　你　想　去　邊　度　呀　？　。

8. Néih jùng-yi sihk māt-yéh a?

　你　鍾　意　食　乜　嘢　呀　？

Listening Exercise

I.

1. *c*　　2. *b*　　3. *a*　　4. *a*　　5. *d*

II.

1. M̀h-haih 唔係　　　2. sei-go 四個　　　3. 1:30

4. móuh 冇　　　　　5. hóu 好　　　　　6. 3:00

LESSON 11

Review Exercise — Translation

1. M̀h-gòi béi nī-bún syù ngóh.

　唔　該　畀　呢　本　書　我　。

2. Ngóh móuh heui gó-douh.

　我　冇　去　嗰　度　。

3. Ngóh pàhng-yáuh kàhm-máahn sahp-yāt-dím-sàam fan-gaau.

　我　朋　友　琴　晚　十　一　點　三　瞓　覺　。

4. M̀h-gòi béi gàm-yaht ge bou-jí kéuih.
   唔　該　畀　今　日　嘅　報　紙　佢　。

5. Kéuih taai-táai m̀h-sái máaih-yéh.
   佢　太　太　唔　駛　買　嘢　。

6. Ngóh yám-jó léuhng bùi chàh.
   我　飲　咗　兩　杯　茶　。

7. Néih béi jì bāt bīn-go a?
   你　畀　枝　筆　邊　個　呀　？

8. Ngóh béi-jó sahp jèung jí néih.
   我　畀　咗　十　張　紙　你　。

9. Ngóh tìng-yaht yiu fàan ūk-kéi sihk-faahn.
   我　聽　日　要　返　屋　企　食　飯　。

10. Ngóh-deih móuh daap chè
    我　哋　冇　搭　車　。

Listening Exersise

1. *a*　2. *c*　3. *c*　4. *d*　5. *b*　6. *d*　7. *a*　8. *c*

LESSON 12

Review Exercise

I.　Rewrite Sentences

1. Ngóh ge sé-jih-làuh hái sahp-baat láu.
   我　嘅　寫　字　樓　喺　十　八　樓　。

2. Néih hái bīn-douh jyuh a?
   你　喺　邊　度　住　呀　？

3. Nī-gàan gūng-sī m̀h-hái jùng-wàahn.

呢 間 公 司 唔 喺 中 環 。

4. Bīn-go hái Wāan-jái fàan-gùng a?

邊 個 喺 灣 仔 返 工 呀 ?

5. Ngóh ge pàhng-yáuh hái Jìm-sà-jéui jyuh.

我 嘅 朋 友 喺 尖 沙 咀 住 。

6. Léih sìn-sàang hái sàam láu yám chàh.

李 先 生 喺 三 樓 飲 茶 。

7. Ngóh m̀h-hái Tùhng-lòh-wāan jyuh.

我 唔 喺 銅 鑼 灣 住 。

II. Translation

1. Néih jùng m̀h-jùng-yi nī-gāan jáu-làuh a?

你 鍾 唔 鍾 意 呢 間 酒 樓 呀 ?

2. Ngóh hái Jìm-sà-jéui jyuh.

我 喺 尖 沙 咀 住 。

3. Néih pàhng-yáuh hái bīn-douh jouh-yéh a?

你 朋 友 喺 邊 度 做 嘢 呀 ?

4. Ngóh gàm-yaht hái ūk-kéi sihk-faahn.

我 今 日 喺 屋 企 食 飯 。

5. Néih léuhng-dím-bun hái bīn-douh a?

你 兩 點 半 喺 邊 度 呀 ?

6. Ngóh sé-jih-làuh hái yah-ńg h láu.

我 寫 字 樓 喺 廿 五 樓 。

7. Ngóh tùhng pàhng-yáuh hái Wāan-jái sihk-faahn.

我 同 朋 友 喺 灣 仔 食 飯 。

8. Chàhn sìn-sàang kàhm-yaht hái bīn-douh a?
   陳　先　生　琴　日　喺　邊　度　呀？

9. Ngóh heui Tùhng-lòh-wāan máaih-yéh.
   我　去　銅　鑼　灣　買　嘢。

10. Néih sé-jih-làuh hái bīn-douh a?
    你　寫　字　樓　喺　邊　度　呀？

11. Néih-deih géi-dím hái mùhn-háu dáng a?
    我　哋　幾　點　喺　門　口　等　呀？

12. Ngóh taai-táai ge sé-jih-làuh m̀h-hái Gàm-jùng.
    我　太　太　嘅　寫　字　樓　唔　喺　金　鐘。

III.

1. m̀h-haih, haih B1
   唔係，係 B1

2. yih láu 二樓

3. haih 係

4. ngāam 啱

5. B1

6. móuh tùhng-jōng 冇童裝

7. yáuh 有

8. ngāam 啱

9. luhk láu 六樓

10. ńgh láu 五樓

Listening Exercise

I.

1. Gām-jūng 金鐘

2. máaih-yéh 買嘢

3. pàhng-yáuh 朋友

4. hóu 好

5. Tùhng-lòh-wāan 銅鑼灣

6. yám chàh 飲茶

7. m̀h-dāk-hàahn 唔得閒

8. fàan-gùng 返工

II.

  1. *a*   2. *b*   3. *d*

LESSON 13

A. Days of the Week — Practice

1. 18°C	5. 25°C	9. 17°C
2. 20°C	6. m̀h-haih 唔係	10. m̀h-haih 唔係
3. 32°C	7. haih 係	
4. 22°C	8. m̀h-haih 唔係	

B. Date — Practice

II.

  1. hóu-tìn 好天

  2. móuh 冇

  3. m̀h-haih 唔係，lohk-yúh 落雨

  4. haih 係

  5. m̀h-haih 唔係，lohk-yúh 落雨

  6. m̀h-haih 唔係，hóu-tìn 好天

  7. yih-saph-houh hóu-tìn 二十號好天，
daahn-haih yih-saph-sei-houh yàm-tìn 但係二十四號陰天

  8. móuh 冇

  9. hóu-tìn 好天

10. m̀h-haih 唔係，tīng-yaht lohk-yúh 聽日落雨

Review Exercise

I. Rewrite sentences

1. Ngóh luhk-yuht heui-jó léuih-hàhng.

    我 六 月 去 咗 旅 行 。

2. Nī-go láih-baai-sàam sei-dím hòi-wúi.

    呢 個 禮 拜 三 四 點 開 會 。

3. Kàhm-yaht hóu m̀h-hóu-tìn a?

    琴 日 好 唔 好 天 呀 ？

4. Ngóh sìng-kèih yih m̀h-dāk-hàahn, daahn-haih sìng-
    kèih-sei dāk-hàahn.

    我 星 期 二 唔 得 閒 ， 但 係 星 期 四 得 閒 。

5. Ngóh-deih tìng-yaht heui léuih-hàhng hóu m̀h-hóu a?

    我 哋 聽 日 去 旅 行 好 唔 好 呀 ？

6. Gàm-yaht ge tìn-hei hóu syù-fuhk.

    今 日 嘅 天 氣 好 舒 服 。

II. Translation

1. Yìng-màhn syù gwai-gwo yìng-màhn bou-jí hóu-dò.

    英 文 書 貴 過 英 文 報 紙 好 多 。

2. Seuhng-go láih-baai móuh lohk-yúh.

    上 個 禮 拜 冇 落 雨 。

3. Sìng-kèih-yāt hòi-wúi, daahn-haih ngóh m̀h-dāk-hàahn
    heui.

    星 期 一 開 會 ， 但 係 我 唔 得 閒 去 。

4. Néih hah-go sìng-kèih-luhk heui bīn-douh a?

    你 下 個 星 期 六 去 邊 度 呀 ？

5. Yāt-yuht hóu dung, chāt-yuht hóu yiht.

    一 月 好 凍 ， 七 月 好 熱 。

6. Ngóh yáuh-sìh tùhng tùhng-sih sihk aan, yáuh-sìh tùhng
   pàhng-yàuh sihk.

   我 有 時 同 同 事 食 晏 ， 有 時 同 朋 友
   食 。

7. Sìng-kéih-ńgh hóu hóu-tìn, daahn-haih sìng-kèih-luhk
   lohk yúh.

   星 期 五 好 好 天 ， 但 係 星 期 六 落
   雨 。

8. Ngóh sìh -sìh hái sé-jih-làuh sihk aan.

   我 時 時 喺 寫 字 樓 食 晏 。

9. Sei-yuht yah-sàam houh fong m̀h-fong-ga a?

   四 月 廿 三 號 放 唔 放 假 呀 ？

10. Ngóh sìng-kèih-yāt ji ńgh fàan-gùng. Sìng-kèih-luhk
    heui máaih-yéh. Sìng-kèih-yaht hái ūk-kéi fan-gaau.

    我 星 期 一 至 五 返 工 。 星 期 六 去
    買 嘢 。 星 期 日 喺 屋 企 瞓 覺 。

11. Seuhng-go sìng-kèih-yih yàm-tìn.

    上 個 星 期 二 陰 天 。

12. Sahp-yāt-yuht ge tìn-hei hóu syù-fuhk.

    十 一 月 嘅 天 氣 好 舒 服 。

Listening Exercise

1. láih-baai-sàam 禮拜三
2. 30°C
3. sìng-kèih-yāt 星期一
4. haih 係
5. haih 係
6. fan-gaau 瞓覺
7. fan-gaau 瞓覺
8. m̀h-hóu 唔好
9. móuh 冇
10. màh-má-déi 麻麻哋

LESSON 14

Practice

1. Ngóh jì sahp-ńgh láu yáuh yāt gāan chāan-tēng.

   我 知 十 五 樓 有 一 間 餐 廳。

2. Kéuih sīk ngóh pàhng-yáuh.

   佢 識 我 朋 友。

3. Ngóh m̀h-jì Hàhng-sāng Ngàhn-hòhng hái bīn-douh.

   我 唔 知 恒 生 銀 行 喺 邊 度。

4. Ngóh m̀h-sīk heui gó-douh.

   我 唔 識 去 嗰 度。

5. Néih sīk m̀h-sīk Yìng-màhn a?

   你 識 唔 識 英 文 呀？

6. Ngóh m̀h-sīk tái jùng-màhn bou-jí

   我 唔 識 睇 中 文 報 紙。

Review Exercise

I. Fill in the blanks

1. sīk, sīk 識，識

2. Yùh-gwó, jauh
   如果，就

3. deih-tit 地鐵

4. Yùh-gwó, jauh 如果，就

5. jauh fan-gaau 就瞓覺

6. Yùh-gwó m̀h-sihk jóu-chāan
   如果唔食早餐

II. Translation

1. Ngóh tùhng-sih hái fuk-gahn jyuh.

   我 同 事 喺 附 近 住。

2. Ngóh m̀h-sīk Wòhng sìn-sàang.

我 唔 識 黃 先 生 。

3. yùh-gwó néih séung máaih Yìng-màhn syù, heui gó-gāan pou-táu máaih lā.

如 果 你 想 買 英 文 書 ， 去 嗰 間 舖 頭 買 啦 。

4. Ngóh jì kéuih haih Léih taai-táai ge pàhng-yáuh.

我 知 佢 係 李 太 太 嘅 朋 友 。

5. Lip hái mùhn-háu ge hauh-mihn.

軪 喺 門 口 嘅 後 面 。

6. Ngóh hái gó-gàan ngàhn-hòhng chìhn-mihn daap dīk-sí.

我 喺 嗰 間 銀 行 前 面 搭 的 士 。

7. Jùng-wàahn yáuh hóu-dò hóu ge chāan-tēng.

中 環 有 好 多 好 嘅 餐 廳 。

8. Seuhng-mihn yáuh jáu-dim.

上 面 有 酒 店 。

9. Kéuih hái Tùhng-lòh-wāan fuh-gahn jyuh.

佢 喺 銅 鑼 灣 附 近 住 。

10. Nī-douh móuh síu-bā.

呢 度 冇 小 巴 。

IV.

1. jó-mihn 左面

2. sé-jih-làuh ge deui-mihn 寫字樓嘅對面

3. pou-táu ge jó-mihn 舖頭嘅左面

4. yauh-mihn 右面

5. yáuh 有

6. jáu-táu ge hauh-mihn 酒樓嘅後面

7. syù-dim ge deui-mihn 書店嘅對面

8. syù-dim, hái sé-jih-làuh ge yauh-mihn
   書店，喺寫字樓嘅右面

9. jó-mihn 左面

10. pou-táu ge hauh-mihn 舖頭嘅後面

11. móuh 冇

12. jó-mihn 左面

Listening Exercise

1. sīk 識   2. tùhng-sih 同事   3. haih 係

4. m̀h-haih 唔係   5. yauh-mihn 右面   6. yáuh 有

7. Taai-gwú Gwóng-chèuhng 太古廣場

8. deui-mihn 對面   9. m̀h-haih 唔係

10. Hèung-góng jáu-dim 香港酒店   11. 8:00

12. Tùhng-lòh-wāan deih-tit-jaahm Hàhng-sāng Ngàhn-hòhng
    銅 鑼 灣 地 鐵 站 恆 生 銀 行

LESSON 15

Review Exercise

I. Translation

1. Ngóh pàhng-yáuh wúih hohk Gwóng-dùng-wá.
   我 朋 友 會 學 廣 東 話 。

2. Néih jouh-gán māt-yéh a?
   你 做 緊 乜 嘢 呀 ?

3. Ngóh jouh-gán yéh, ngóh chìh-dī dá dihn-wá béi néih.

   我 做 緊 嘢 ，我 遲 啲 打 電 話 畀 你 。

4. Néih dáng-jó ngóh géi-noih la?

   你 等 咗 我 幾 耐 喇 ？

5. Ngóh hái nī-douh sàam-nìhn la.

   我 喺 呢 度 三 年 喇 。

6. Néih tùhng bīn-go kìng-gán a?

   你 同 邊 個 傾 緊 呀 ？

7. Néih sihk aan sihk géi-noih ga?

   你 食 晏 食 幾 耐 㗎 ？

8. Néih máaih-jó nī-go dihn-sih géi-noih a?

   你 買 咗 呢 個 電 視 幾 耐 呀 ？

9. Néih pìhng-sìh dāk-hàahn jouh māt-yéh a?

   你 平 時 得 閒 做 乜 嘢 呀 ？

10. Ngóh nám-jó yāt fàn-jùng.

    我 諗 咗 一 分 鐘 。

11. Sìng-kèih-ngh wúih m̀h-wúih lohk-yúh a?

    星 期 五 會 唔 會 落 雨 呀 ？

12. Ngóh sìng-kèih-yaht wúih heui Jìm-sà-jéui máaih yéh. Néih làih m̀h-làih a?

    我 星 期 日 會 去 尖 沙 咀 買 嘢 。 你
    嚟 唔 嚟 呀 ？

III. Review on 'yih' 二 and 'léuhng' 兩

1. léuhng nìhn 兩年

2. léuhng-dím-yih 兩點二

3. yāt-yuht yih houh 一月二號

4. léuhng go jùng-tàuh yih-sahp fàn-jùng
   兩個鐘頭二十分鐘

5. léuhng-go-yih 兩個二

6. sìng-kèih-yih 星期二 / láih-baai-yih 禮拜二

7. yih-yuht 二月

8. léuhng hòuh-jí 兩毫子

9. yih-sahp-yih go yàhn 二十二個人

10. yih-lìhng-lìhng-yih-nìhn 二零零二年

11. léuhng mān 兩蚊

12. yih chìn jèung jí 二千張紙

13. yāt-gáu-gáu-yih nìhn yih-yuht yih houh
    一九九二年二月二號

14. yih-baak-lìhng-yih fàn-jùng 二百零二分鐘

15. yih-baak yāt-sahp-yih go yuht 二百一十二個月

16. yih-baat-go sìng-kèih 二百個星期

LESSON 16

Review Exercise

I. Translation

1. Néih heui-gwo gó-gàan jáu-làuh yám-chàh meih a?
    你 去 過 嗰 間 酒 樓 飲 茶 未 呀？

2. Ngóh gei-dāk, daahn-haih ngóh meih jouh.
    我 記 得，但 係 我 未 做。

3. Néih daap-gwo deih-tit heui Jùng-wàahn meih a?
    你 搭 過 地 鐵 去 中 環 未 呀？

4. Ngóh meih heui-gwo néih ūk-kéi.

我 未 去 過 你 屋 企 。

5. Kéuih m̀h-syù-fuhk. Kéuih gàm-yaht m̀h-hòi-dāk-wúi.

佢 唔 舒 服 。 佢 今 日 唔 開 得 會 。

6. Nī-yeuhng yéh tìhm dihng hàahm ga?

呢 樣 嘢 甜 定 鹹 㗎 ？

7. Néih sihk sìn lā. Ngóh m̀h-tóuh-ngoh.

你 食 先 啦 。 我 唔 肚 餓 。

8. Ngóh yiu tèng dihn-wá sìn. Ngóh-deih chìh-dī kìng.

我 要 聽 電 話 先 。 我 哋 遲 啲 傾 。

9. Nī-douh m̀h-jihk-heui-dāk. Néih yiu jyun jó.

呢 度 唔 直 去 得 。 你 要 轉 左 。

10. Ngóh meih gin-gwo kéuih. Kéuih haih bīn-go a?

我 未 見 過 佢 。 佢 係 邊 個 呀 ？

11. Kéuih meih fàan-làih.

我 佢 未 返 嚟 。

12. Néih yáuh móuh tái-gwo gó-tou hei a? Ngóh tái-gwo léuhng chi.

你 有 冇 睇 過 套 戲 ？ 我 睇 過 兩 次 。